Ordnance Survey 1:2500 plan (1st edition 1872).

ASH

———◆———

AN EAST KENT VILLAGE

The Street, *c.*1890.

ASH

An East Kent Village

David Downes

Phillimore

2000

Published by
PHILLIMORE & CO. LTD.
Shopwyke Manor Barn, Chichester, West Sussex

ISBN 1 86077 134 3

Printed and bound in Great Britain by
The Cromwell Press
Trowbridge

CONTENTS

LIST OF ILLUSTRATIONS

Frontispiece: The Street, *c*.1890

FOREWORD

In putting this book together I have been helped and encouraged over many years by more people than I can hope even to remember.

Nobody exploring the history of Ash can escape being deeply indebted to the work nearly 150 years ago of James Robinson Planché which resulted in the publication in 1864 of his *A Corner of Kent*. He was a herald, a professional genealogist, an expert in armour, and writing in more spacious days than the present. He was so good that he is infuriating. Time and again you make an exciting 'new' historical discovery— only to find that it's already in 'Planché'! This book can only hope to complement, not to replace, his.

I must mention here by name just three others: first, the late James Ogilvie, who insisted on giving me my first anti-tetanus jab, to ward off the effects of any accidental encounter with a sardine-tin in a trench on the way down to Iron-Age or Roman remains; secondly, Anthea Newman, who made the voluminous Ash poor law records her own territory; and thirdly, Elizabeth Hudson, whose archive researches brought the exploits of Nathaniel Crosyar, John Love and John Finney, and so much more, to light. A great deal in this book owes everything to them. The responsibility for its undoubted defects, and the many errors which it certainly still contains, is mine alone. I hope my friends will take pleasure in pointing them out to me.

Finally, I must record my grateful thanks to the members of the Ash Parish Council, past and present. This book would never have been written without their encouragement, and without the Council's financial support it could not have been published.

DAVID DOWNES

Ash, March 2000

LIST OF SUBSCRIBERS

Peter G. Adams
Alfred Alexander
Brian and Judith Allpress
Ash Parish Council
The Askew family
John and Gill Aust
Mr. and Mrs. Ayles
To Barb and Mick
Pamela and Norman Baldock
Revd. Clive C. Barlow [Incumbent 1977-1992]
The Reverend David Barnes
Ian and David Bartlett
Barbara Barton and Gaybrielle Barton
Frank Bates
Denis and Pauline Beer
Graham and Penelope Beer
Ivan K. Beer
David and Anne Bennett
Meg Bennetts
John and Yvonne Betts
F.G. Bird
Denis and Marian Blaxland
Martin J. Booty
Alan Bradley
Michael Brady
Mr. B. Brisley
Mr. A.R. Brown
Robert Buddle
Michael Bunce
Joyce Burge
Sally and Ken Burke
Mrs. Grace Burville
Doris Butcher (née Harvey)
M. and N. Byrne
Penelope Campbell
Canterbury Cathedral Library
B.A. Cartwright
Ian and Ruth Castle
Ivan R. Castle
Jack Castle
Steve, Cherrie and Carys Chadwick
Chan's family
Philip G. Chandler
Robert S. Chandler
William and Daphne Chandler
John and Anne Chapman

Janet E. Clarke
Priscilla Jane Clarke
W.A. Clarke
Rick and Ann Clemence
Mr. and Mrs. David Cleverdon
Alan Collard
E.A. Coltham
Robin and Addie Colyer
Joyce L. Cudworth
Mrs. Janet S. Dale
Mrs. Monica Davies
Patricia Ann Deveson
Enid Douglas (née Elvey)
Petula Draper
Mr. Eric Driscoll
Mrs. Pat Dunn
Dr. Christopher Dutton
Neil and Andrea Dymant
Mr. C.G. Ende
Trevor and Mary Evans
Dr. J.G. Everett
Peter and Lynne Ewart
Richard and Julia Farbrace
Ferne/Greenwood
Janice Field
Mrs. Gladys Finch
Mr. Harry Finch
Andrew and Rachel Fleetwood
Graham Foat
Alan Fordham
Tom Gardener
Anita Gavin
Maurice George Gilbert
Mrs. M.J. Gillanders
Mr. E.D. Goatham
Mr. W.D. Goatham
Graham and Linda Goodwin
Sarah Gordon
Jim Graves
Nicola Greaves
Rev. Canon Gerald Greenwood
Josephine Griffiths
Vaughan Grylls
A.N. Gunn, Esq.
Mr. Laurence F. Hammond
Jean and Eric Hands

Heather Harle
Mrs. Ann J. Harris
Mary Hayward
Doreen Heyes
Craig, Kath and Ashley Hooker
David Hooker
Mr. and Mrs. David Hopper
P.M. Horn
Bill Hougham
John Hougham
Jim and Elizabeth Hudson
Pat Hume
Anita Humpston
Rhona M. Hunter
Derek and Margery Hyde
Geoffrey L. Jackson
E. Jarvis (Mrs.)
To Jean from David
Susan and Tony Johnson
Tony Jones
Mr. K.C.D. and Mrs. Valerie Jordan
Marjorie O. Kimberley
Mrs. Glenys Kirk
A. Knight
C. Knight
D.E. Knight
K.E. Knight
Peter and Patricia Knott
Mr. A.D. Laker
D.F. and M.M. Lampard
Dulcie Larkins
Bill and Linda Laslett
Gary William Laslett
Frederick and Olive Ledner
To Lesley and Geoff
Eileen Lilley
Adam Limbrey
The Lion Hotel
Mrs. David McCabe
Dr. N. and Mrs. M. McCanch
David and Toni McEwen
Dr. Sara Maclennan (née Connell)
Kevin and Cheryl Magill
Alison Martin
Dave and Pam Mawson
Nigel and Sarah Miller
Mrs. Kathleen Mills
James and Marie Milne
Lesley P. Munro
Brian John Murrum and family
David and Alison Nicholass
Brian and Eunice O'Kelly
The Old Rectory Residential Home
Paul W. Osborne
Richard and Carole Palmer
D. Philpott
Mr. and Mrs. Derek Pilcher
Jean Poile
Chris and Ursula Pratt

Mr. and Mrs. W.B. Preston
Sylvia Profitt
J.S. Rajan
Bill Ralph
Cyril J. Ralph
Tony and Philippa Redding
Gillian Rickard
Ben Ring and Jayne Dunsbee
Julian A.D. Roberts
Dr. and Mrs. S.J. Robinson, Maxwell and Harriet
Mr. and Mrs. K. Rogers and family
Mrs. Winifred Rolfe
David Ross
Evelyn Maureen Rumley (née Richards)
Janet, Jade and Krystal Rumley
J.H. Ryan
S.G. Castle Builders
Ivy May Sackett
Dolly and Bernard Sampson
Irene Sandford
Eric M. Satterley C.Eng F.I.Mar.E. and Ann M. Satterley
N.P. Shimmin
In memory of Harold G. Shoebridge
Cheryl Shorter
Carole Slone
Pat and Peggy Smalley
Wendy Smissen
Mr. and Mrs. D.J. Smith
Cllr. Mrs. Mary Smith
Tim Smith
Michael G. Stewart
D. Kim Stillman and Mr. Thomas F. Farling
Elizabeth Anne Sutton
Ann Talbert
Colin and Linda Tappenden
Graham Tappenden
Phyllis Tappenden (née Miles)
Marion Tickner
Simon Tickner
Mrs. Julie Turmaine
Joan and Tony Turner
Mrs. S. Turner
Charles Turp
Mrs. Joan Upton
Joyce and Jerry Uwins
Alexandra Lauren van Dijk
Simon Vinson
Rita Wale
Jill Warley
Mr. and Mrs. B.G. Wayte
Mr. Ernest William Henry Wellard
Ned, Hazel and Jack West-Sherring
Nigel Whitburn
Carol and Paul Wilkinson
Patricia and James Wilkinson
Barbara Williams-Jones
Ted and Jessie Willis
Mr. Graham Wraight

INTRODUCTION

The parish of Ash is one of the largest in Kent, 7,011 acres in extent, on the road between the cathedral city of Canterbury and the old Cinque Port of Sandwich, nine miles from the city and three from Sandwich. To its north and east, the parish is bounded by the tidal, though narrow, river Stour. The wide, marshland pastures of the Ash Level have for at least 700 years provided about 3,000 acres of first-class grazing for cattle and sheep, though much of it is now under the plough. The south-western part of the parish, once a huge sandbank left by the sea, on which the main village and the several smaller hamlets have grown up, is higher, drier, and richly fertile— the 'black pebble land' of the Thanet and Woolwich Beds. There are still many orchards, soft-fruit plantations and market gardens, though their area is now in decline.

More than a century ago, in 1864, Planché wrote, in his *A Corner of Kent*, 'In historical associations, in archaeological interest, few parishes in the United Kingdom perhaps can equal, and certainly none surpass, that of Ash next Sandwich.' But Ash is not a picture-postcard village. As Dorothy Gardiner wrote in 1934, 'Its history is more like a treasure hoard, hidden and close-kept.'

Undoubtedly the parish is full of history. On a hill in its far north-east corner is the third-century Roman fortress of Richborough Castle, a 'Saxon Shore' fort sited so as to command the eastern entrance of the Wantsum channel between the mainland of Kent and the Isle of Thanet and the main sea-route from the continent to Britain. It may well have been within its massive walls that King Ethelbert met Augustine in A.D. 597, a meeting which sparked the re-conversion of England to Christianity. At Guilton, at the western end of the village, excavations in the 18th century and since have revealed parts of a rich sixth-century Jutish burial ground, many of the finds from which are in the British and Ashmolean Museums, and in others at Liverpool and Canterbury.

Large though the parish is, it once formed just part of the great manor of Wingham belonging to the archbishops of Canterbury, and was created a separate parish only in 1282. About that time a causeway, still existing, was built across the marshes to Sandwich, then at the height of its importance as a Cinque Port. Ash's fortunes were linked with those of Sandwich, and the more substantial houses in the parish were often peopled by wealthy merchants of Sandwich and Calais. In 1364 Lord Latimer was granted a royal licence to hold a weekly market at Ash, which became, therefore, for a time at least, a little market town in its own right. But by the reign of Queen Elizabeth I—partly because of the 'inning' and draining of the

Ash marshes—Sandwich's haven had silted up, and it soon became 'a sad old town, all timber building'. Ash, too, resumed life as a village. But perhaps as a result of its short life as a market town, unlike so many country parishes it has never fallen into the hands of a single landowner, or even a very few large owners. Perhaps also as a result, there has long been a strong free church tradition in the parish. In the troubled years of the 17th-century religious feelings here ran high, and successive ministers were ejected and restored. It may be from that time that there has come down the cynical couplet, certainly more than 200 years old:

> Ash church with its peaked steeple,
>
> A bad parson and worse people.

Eighty years ago, in the early, headily optimistic days of the Kent coalfield, Ash almost became an industrial village. But the rich soil of the parish has long been highly prized. The medieval archbishops' home farm—the 'barton'—on their Wingham manor was at 'Wingham Barton' in Ash parish. The pattern of agriculture here has changed much even during the 20th century. But farming is still, as it has always been, the rock on which the prosperity of the parish rests, and at the end of the century it is in crisis again.

ONE

BEFORE THE ROMANS

What is now east Kent finally emerged from the sea about 40 million years ago. Much earlier, about 300 million years ago, forests had decayed to form the present coal seams, now deep down beneath the thick chalk which gradually covered them during some 70 million years beneath the sea. For another 30 million years the sea alternately invaded and retreated from the new chalk land, leaving behind sea-washed flints and sand.

The Ice Ages began about two million years ago. Great ice-sheets spread and melted four times. They never reached further south than what is now Essex, but what is now east Kent was intensely cold. Above permanently frozen ground, during at least one period of relatively moist climate a layer of chalk annually froze and thawed, allowing sandy, chalky rubble to slip down into the valleys. About 250,000 years ago there lived in what is now Kent the earliest known Briton. Her remains, three skull bones, discovered separately in 1935, 1936 and 1955, from one young woman, were found at Swanscombe. Other rare traces in Kent of these Neanderthal people include part of a deer antler and a piece of elephant bone—probably from animals killed for food—and flint hand-axes intended as cutting tools. Much later, during the earlier part of the final Ice Age which began about 75,000 years ago, rock-shelters were shared by 'cave-men' with wild animals such as mammoth, woolly rhino and giant elk. In 1961 a tusk and bones of a mammoth were found in gravel, five feet below the present road, at Claypits in Goodnestone, 2½ miles south-west of Ash village.

During a period of cold, very dry climate, about 25,000 years ago, fierce winds carried silt from Eastern Europe westwards as far as what is now south-east England. Much of this dust, known as brick-earth, was deposited in east Kent. Life in Britain was almost wiped out in this last Ice Age. Only the kind of plants now found on mountain-tops, very few larger animals, and almost certainly no men, survived even in the south. Meanwhile, Neanderthal men had died out everywhere. In their place, about 40,000 years ago, 'modern' men, physically just like people living today, spread to nearly all parts of the world. They lived mainly by hunting large animals in big, organised groups. But they were also artists, creating magnificent cave-paintings and carving human figures, so they probably knew how to use language.

Water was drawn from the sea to form great ice-sheets, and shallows became dry land. As the ice melted, sea-level rose to flood low-lying areas. A river flowed northwards, through what are now the Straits of Dover and across a plain which occupied the southern part of the present North Sea, to join the Thames and Rhine before reaching the sea. Twice, advancing glaciers held back the waters so that they overspilled southwards through the Straits. Finally, as the melting ice caused the sea-level to rise again, the sea advanced up the Straits, leaving the Dogger Bank further north as a last land-bridge between Britain and continental Europe. About 7600 B.C., the Straits of Dover and the southern North Sea formed a narrow channel some 10 miles wide, into which the Rhine and the Thames both flowed, with sea-level about 130 feet lower than today. By about 7300 B.C. sea-level had risen enough to flood the channels of the Thames, the Medway, the Swale, and the Stour. About 6600 B.C. the Dogger Bank land-bridge was breached, so that Britain became entirely separated from the Continent. By 6000 B.C. the shore-line of north-east Kent was very like today's, but the Isle of Thanet was much larger, erosion having since reduced its size. Then, and for long afterwards, it was a true island, cut off from Kent by the Wantsum, an arm of the sea stretching from the Thames estuary east of Reculver in the north to the English channel at Pegwell Bay in the east. The river Stour flowed into the Wantsum near the place still called Stourmouth.

Meanwhile, as long as the land-bridge from the Continent existed, plants, animals and men could all follow the melting ice back into Britain. As the climate grew warmer, arctic birch and scrub gave way to pine forest; then hazel, alder, oak and lime spread northwards. By 5500 B.C. southern England was a land of dense, mixed oak forest.

Early men were nomads and hunters, but their number was steadily increasing and in many areas there were fewer large animals to hunt. Men following a new way of life, farmers who cultivated their land and grew and herded their food, slowly spread from the Mediterranean. Farming probably developed to meet a shortage of food; from any given area of land farmers could produce much more food than hunters could kill or gather. By 3000 B.C. they had reached Britain, bringing with them pottery and polished stone tools. A polished stone axe, and an arrowhead have been found on Richborough hill, in Ash. Another flint axe and arrowhead were found with some pottery in 1992 at Each End, during a 'rescue' excavation before the construction of the Ash by-pass. Scattered struck flints, unworked, from about this period were found, also in 1992, during salvage archaeological recordings at Millfield in Ash. Between Stourmouth and Preston, and at Wingham, animal bones and an antler-comb, probably used to dress skins, were found in a pit very likely intended as a granary. By this time at least some of the forest around Ash had been cut down, and there was open land, both arable and pasture.

About 2000 B.C. new immigrants, skilled in working in metal—first copper, then bronze—followed. Traces of them (called, from the red pottery drinking vessels they made, 'Beaker' people) have been discovered in at least 12 places in Kent, including an arrowhead and part of a bronze axe at Richborough, a beaker at Wingham, and 'incense cups' at Tilmanstone and Bekesbourne. At Hoaden in Ash, in 1974 and 1983, 114 pieces from a bronze-smith's stock of about 900 B.C.—including five bronze axes (three of which were made in Gaul), a spear head, 22 fragments of sword-blades, 18 fragments of axes, five fragments of spear-head, pieces of tools, and ingots—were found. About 1994 a bronze sword of the same period was found at Shatterling, a mile south of Hoaden. The Beaker people also brought to Britain with them simple ploughs, which made it possible to till heavier, clay soils.

The technique of working in iron—more difficult than in bronze—spread from Turkey across Europe to Britain by 650 B.C. Once the skills had been mastered, iron

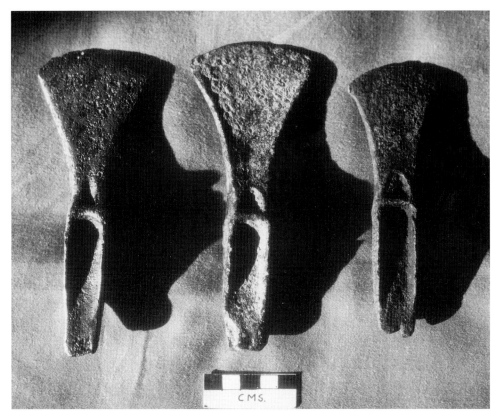

1 Bronze-Age axes found in a field at Hoaden in 1974, part of a much larger find (photograph by J.D. Ogilvie).

ore was much more widely available than copper or tin, and used not only for weapons but also for agricultural implements. A series of ditches forming part of an Early Iron-Age farmstead, perhaps surrounded by a defensive palisade, was found on Richborough hill, as well as at least three occupation sites from this period along the ridge from Stourmouth through Preston to Wingham, and in 1992 another at Millfield, Ash. Between 100 and 75 B.C. there was another wave of immigrants from northern France. The new arrivals, the Belgae, were refugees from the Roman conquest of Gaul. They brought with them wheel-turned pottery, coinage and more efficient ploughs.

The Mediterranean lands, enjoying a sub-tropical climate, became the cradle of European civilisation. But the Greeks cut down their broad-leaved woodlands and, worse, domesticated the wild goat. Herds of goats, browsers rather than grazers, ate vegetation down to the ground, stripped foliage from trees, and prevented any regeneration. Erosion by wind and rain followed. The Romans learned nothing from the Greeks' disastrous experience. Slowly, much of the Mediterranean countryside was reduced to 'maquis', shrubs and low evergreen trees, or even to barren desert. As a result, to provide food for Rome itself the Romans found themselves compelled to extend their boundaries ever wider, and in 55 B.C. they turned towards Britain, and the cornfields of east Kent.

Two

RICHBOROUGH:
GATEWAY TO ROMAN BRITAIN

Julius Caesar's scouts, sent ahead to reconnoitre the British coast, failed to discover the harbour of Richborough. When, on 25 August 55 B.C.—the first absolute date in British history—Caesar crossed the Channel, he ran his ships ashore on an open beach near Walmer. A storm badly damaged them, and scattered the following transports carrying the cavalry. Caesar dared not press forward inland so that, although the Britons quickly made peace, this expedition was not the success for which he had hoped. Next year, 54 B.C., his expedition to Britain was on a much larger scale. He landed unopposed, again on an open beach, between Deal and Sandwich, about 7 July. He reached the Stour next morning, drove the Britons from the river-crossing on the site of modern Canterbury, captured their hill-fort at Bigbury, waded across the Thames, and finally captured their headquarters at Wheathampstead in Hertfordshire. He spent two months in Britain, but left probably still not knowing that the sheltered harbour at Richborough existed.

The Wantsum channel was by this time already partly blocked at its eastern end by a shingle bank at Stonor, which acted as a breakwater to protect the Richborough harbour from storms. Probably there were two eastern entrances into the Wantsum, north and south of the shingle bank. Perhaps Richborough itself was already no longer a true island but, like Reculver at the north mouth of the Wantsum, a peninsula joined to the mainland by a strip of clay marsh. The harbour lay on its seaward side, under the shelter of the Stonar beach.

Eighty-seven years after Caesar's second expedition, the hungry eyes of Imperial Rome again fastened on to the cornfields of Britain, this time bent upon conquest. The campaign in A.D. 43 began about the beginning of May, when an army of about 40,000 men—the IInd, IXth, XIVth and XXth Legions, with auxiliaries—under the command of Aulus Plautius, sailed from Boulogne and landed at Richborough. Quickly securing his beachhead with double ditches, Plautius advanced inland through Kent. He routed the Britons in two skirmishes, and pushed ahead to the Medway and the Thames. The Emperor Claudius himself arrived about the middle of August, bringing with him elephants as well as detachments of his Praetorian Guard and part of the VIIIth Legion, but he stayed in Britain little more than a fortnight.

Although the invasion moved swiftly through Kent, a great military supply base was quickly established at Richborough, with a regular street-plan and large granaries or warehouses. Imports of corn gradually ceased, as supplies from Britain itself increased, and by A.D. 70 the granaries had been replaced by shops and stores. The military base had become a thriving Channel port, *Portus Rutupis.*

About A.D. 85, at the end of Agricola's term as governor of Britain, when its conquest was regarded as complete, craftsmen were brought to Richborough to construct a four-way Triumphal Arch. Built on massive foundations, it had main columns at least 40 feet high and arches 20 feet wide, and was faced with Carrara marble and decorated with bronze statues. Set up at the head of the original Watling Street, the road to London, marking the gateway to Britain from the sea, it was the most elaborate public monument in Roman Britain.

About A.D. 90, after a serious fire, many of the timber buildings at Richborough were rebuilt in stone. But some time after A.D. 100, although Richborough still remained a port of embarkation, the headquarters of the Roman navy, the *Classis Britannicus*, were transferred to the growing port of Dover. Richborough began to decline, and lost much of its trade. Although a town grew up west of the Triumphal Arch, the roads and some of the buildings fell into disrepair. Soon after A.D. 200, marble began to flake off the Arch itself.

Saxon raids on the coast became increasingly frequent. The first of the 'Saxon Shore' forts was built at Reculver, at the northern end of the Wantsum channel, about A.D. 225. At Richborough, about forty years later, probably to answer a sudden emergency, an area about 300 feet square round the Triumphal Arch was surrounded by three ditches and an earth rampart, and the Arch itself adapted to serve as a look-out post against raiders. Suddenly, and significantly, many more hoards of coins began to be deliberately buried. The earth fort was hardly complete when, about A.D. 268, under the direction of Marcus Aurelius Mauseus Carausius, who had established himself in Britain as a separatist emperor, it was replaced by a bigger stone fort, to house a large permanent garrison. Part of Carausius' new coastal defences stretching from the Wash to the Solent,

2 The Saxon Shore Fort at Richborough, *c.*1925 (Office of Works photograph).

3 The Saxon Shore Fort, Richborough, the base of the south-west circular tower, *c.*1850 (engraved by Frederick William Fairchild).

4 The Saxon Shore Fort, Richborough, interior view of postern gate in the north wall, *c.*1850 (engraved by Frederick William Fairchild).

this new Saxon Shore fort, originally intended to be about 500 feet square but lengthened to between 550 and 580 feet, covered more than six acres. Probably it had wide gates flanked by towers on the east and west sides, with narrow postern gates concealed in bastions at each corner. Its massive walls, protected by a surrounding double ditch, were 11 feet thick—and in places still stand 25 feet high. Inside the fort most of the new military buildings were of timber, apart from a stone-built bath-block.

An amphitheatre, about 600 yards south-west of the fort, was constructed as an arena for military games. Bear-baiting, for which live bears were imported from Britain, was a favourite spectacle in the Roman circus; and British oysters were highly esteemed by Roman gourmets. Both bears and oysters were identified with the 'Ritupine shore'.

Richborough continued to be occupied as an important military base, as well as an entry port into Britain. Part of the IVth Legion was stationed here during the fourth century. In A.D. 342 some crisis was sufficiently severe to cause the Emperor Constans to pay a hurried visit. When, following a concerted Saxon attack on Britain in A.D. 367-8, Count Theodosius landed here to restore the situation, Richborough's harbour was described as 'safe and quiet'. Even after A.D. 410, when Roman troops were finally withdrawn, Germans, strengthened by mercenaries, probably remained to guard the fort well into the fifth century. Weapons are not normally found in the graves of Romans, so those discovered in a cemetery at Richborough were probably buried in graves of enlisted barbarian troops.

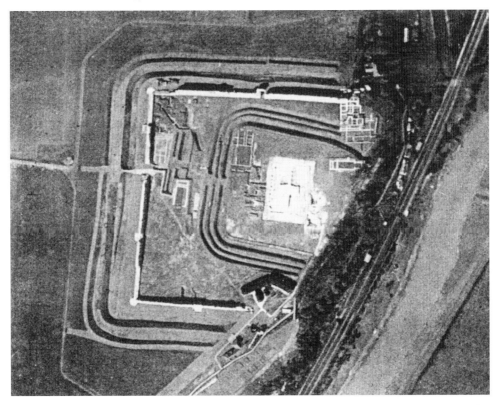

5 The Saxon Shore Fort from the air, Richborough, *c.*1935 (RAF official photograph).

6   The amphitheatre, Richborough, *c*.1720 (engraved by Elisha Kirkall (1682?-1742) after a drawing by William Stukeley (1687-1765)).

About A.D. 280, two pagan temples, 40 and 26 feet square, and each surrounded by a veranda, had been built close together about 450 yards south of the fort. About a hundred years later, both were deliberately despoiled, perhaps in a wave of Christian enthusiasm. Also about A.D. 375, a Christian church, built of timber on masonry foundations, with a rectangular nave, an eastern apse, and probably a north aisle in which was a six-sided font or baptistery, was constructed in the north-east corner of the fort. A pottery bowl and a bronze medallion—each bearing a Christian 'Chi-rho' [$\chi\rho$] symbol, as well as a bronze ring inscribed 'JUSTINE VIVAS IN DEO'—have been found. Continued burials and the absence of any pagan cremation cemetery both suggest that late-Roman Christianity may not have died out at Richborough in the fifth century.

Before the coming of the Romans, roads in east Kent had been ridgeways, un-metalled tracks, taking not the shortest route but the easiest, avoiding thick forest and low-lying marshland. One over Neavy Downs led through modern Wingham to Preston; another ran west from the coast by way of the present Ash Street through Nash to join it. The Romans constructed a whole new system, designed for the rapid deployment of infantry. Their new roads, usually metalled with stone and set on a cambered bank, took the shortest practicable route between two points, careless of gradients. The road from Richborough to London must have been the earliest of all to be built. The *Antonine Itinerary* of about A.D. 200, the first 'road book', listed places and staging posts along most of the roads of the Roman Empire: it prefaced its description of the roads of Britain with a statement of the length of the sea-crossing between Boulogne and Richborough, and the 12-mile stretch between Canterbury and Richborough was the final stage of the 491½-mile long Iter II which began at Hadrian's Wall.

Later, the Richborough road formed just one of several military roads centred on Canterbury, linking Canterbury with each of the Kentish ports—Reculver, Richborough, Dover and Lympne—and each port with its neighbours. The exact lines of those which led west from Richborough and which linked Richborough with Reculver are the two most difficult to identify. The London road has been traced westwards from Richborough, from the west gate of the Saxon Shore fort to a causeway across the narrowest part of the channel—by then, probably already marsh—to the mainland near Fleet Farm. Very likely it then turned south-west towards Cooper Street, and along a line of present-day footpaths to Burford's Alley and The Street, where it forked. The route south-east to Street End and what is now a footpath over Mount Ephraim, led along Coombe Lane and, by a lane now partly abandoned, over Beacon Hill, then followed the line of the ridge to Woodnesborough, where it split again: south to Dover, and east to a villa near Poulders Gardens, Sandwich, which was discovered in 1978. The London road, the western fork through Ash, probably followed the old ridgeway to Four Turnings, where there may have been a choice: either straight on to Wenderton, fording the Little Stour to reach Wickhambreaux, on to Pine Wood west of Littlebourne, and Canterbury; or south-westwards along another ridgeway through Wingham to Neavy Downs, and then west again to Pine Wood and Canterbury. Each change in direction had a reason: to make a convenient junction with another road; to make use of an existing track; or to avoid low marshy ground liable to flood.

John Leland, journeying through England in the 1540s, noted what he saw at Richborough:

Richeboro was, or ever the ryver of Sture dyd turn his botom or old canale, withyn the Isle of Thanet, and by lykelyhod the mayn se cam to the very foot of the castel.

The site of the old town or castel ys wonderful fair apon an hille. The walles which remayn ther yet be in cumpase almost as much as the Tower of London. They have bene very hye, thykke, stronge and wel embateled. The mater of them is flynt, mervelus and long brykes both white and redde after the Britons fascion. The sement was made of se sand and smaul pible. Ther ys a great lyklelyhod that the goodly hil abowte the castel, and especially to Sandwich ward hath bene wel inhabited. Corn groweth on the hille yn mervelus plenty, and yn going to plowgh ther hath owte of mynde bene found and now mo antiquites of Romayne mony then yn any place els of England ...

There is, a good flyte shot fro Ratesburgh toward Sandwich, a great dike caste yn a rownd compas, as yt had bene for fens of menne of warre. The cumpace of the grownd withyn is not much above an acre, and it is very holo by casting up the yearth. They cawle the place there Lytleborough. Withyn the castel is a lytle paroche chirch of S. Augustine, and a heremitage ...

Not far fro the heremitage is a cave wher men have sowt and digged for treasure. I saw yt by candel withyn, and there were conys. Yt was so strait that I had no mynd to crepe far yn.

In the north side of the castel ys a hedde in the walle, now sore defaced with wether. They cawle yt Quene Bertha hede. Nere to that place hard by the wal was a pot of Romayne mony fownd.

The number of Roman coins found at Richborough is very remarkable. During the most recent series of excavations alone, between 1922 and 1938, more than 56,000 coins, including 16 buried hoards, were discovered. Yet on Richborough hill itself hardly any excavation has so far been done outside the walls of the Saxon Shore fort; many Roman remains must still await discovery there. In Ash village, two 'Roman urns' were found near Street End about 1860. In 1936 pottery from a cremation burial of A.D. 175-200 was dug up at Overland. A substantial ditched enclosure, with pottery dating from about A.D. 25-125, was identified at Millfield in 1992. A length of road, with its drainage ditches, aligned north-east and south-west directly to Richborough, was found at Each End in 1992 with, close by, evidence of a small farmstead of A.D. 175-200. On each side of this road was a group of cremation burials of A.D. 200-25, the grave-goods from which included a glass beaker, locally-made flagons, Rhenish beakers, some Samian ware and a lamp. There was a single burial of a woman aged about 40 who was, to judge from the size and nature of her grave, a person of high standing. There were also numerous coins dating from after A.D. 300.

A farm at Wingham, with a bath-house and other buildings dating from about A.D. 100, was still occupied by German mercenaries in the early fifth century. There was another at Sandwich, and one at Wenderton where fourth-century coins and pottery and glass have been found. Pottery has also come from Grove Farm at Woodnesborough and from Dixon's Corner, Sandwich Bay. At Cliff's End, a find of Roman glass and pottery included a wine-jar six feet in circumference. As well as a large quantity of pottery, a cemetery has been identified at Preston, and a potter's kiln at Deerson. A Roman temple was found in Castle Field at Worth in 1925, very like the two excavated at Richborough.

North-east of the present village of Ash, on fertile and easily worked land, close to the Roman settlement on Richborough hill, it may be possible to make out in the present layout of roads and footpaths, parallel and often with right-angled corners (allowing for irregularities grown up over 1,600 years), vestiges of Roman 'smallholdings', laid out in rectangular blocks bounded by un-metalled farm roads, for a colony of settlers, perhaps long-service army 'pensioners'.

Three

The Jutes at Ash and the Coming of St Augustine

During the fifth and sixth centuries, after the Romans had abandoned the Province of Britain, south-east England was invaded by successive waves of Jutes, Angles and Saxons. Many Jutes, from Jutland—modern Denmark—came to Kent. The Anglo-Saxon Chronicle says it was in A.D. 449 that they first entered the Wantsum and landed at Ebbsfleet. Although they fought several battles in Kent, including a bloody and decisive one 'near Ebbsfleet' in 465, they came as settlers rather than as raiders, looking for good farmland near their landing-places, to rear cattle and grow corn as they had done in their homeland, and grouping farmsteads together into hamlets and villages.

The newcomers worshipped their own pagan gods like Woden. It was their custom to place jewellery and other objects useful for the next life in their graves; and it is from their cemeteries that most is known about them. A series of cemeteries has been discovered in east Kent, particularly close to the coast, on both shores of the Wantsum, and near the trackways along which their lines of settlement advanced: at Broadstairs, Ozengell, Minster, Monkton and Sarre; at Bekesbourne, Patrixbourne and Kingston; at Deal and Finglesham. The cemeteries nearly always occur on good soil, often near a natural harbour. But they are usually in places close to villages which have been occupied ever since; as a result, very few of the Jutes' actual habitation sites have been identified. At Ash there were cemeteries at Guilton, known since 1759, and at Millfield, only revealed in 1992, both on the sandy ridge north of the Durlock stream.

In 1759, Bryan Faussett 'happening to be at Ash ... and enquiring whether there were any antiquities in the neighbourhood' was directed to 'a large and deep sandpit' at Guilton where 'for a great many years past ... many antiquities of different sorts have been discovered and picked up'. A workman showed him 'something sticking about 3 or 4 inches out of the sand ... It appeared to me to be nothing more than some piece of stick or some root; but he assured me it was the head of a spear; and said he was certain that there was a grave there'. In only 11 days' digging—in 1760, 1762 and 1763—Faussett excavated 106 Jutish graves at Guilton. Passing through Ash in 1773, James Douglas 'observed some children looking with much eagerness among the sand in the pit. On enquiry they told me they were picking up glass beads, several of which I received from them'.

7 A worked and chased silver-gilt girdle-buckle of *c*.600, found in June 1760 by Bryan Faussett, in the Jutish cemetery at Guilton.

8 A square silver-gilt ornament depicting a bird, perhaps part of a clasp, of *c*.600, found in 1760 by Faussett, at Guilton.

9 A brass buckle with figures of two four-legged creatures of *c*.600, found in August 1763 by Faussett, at Guilton.

The cemetery at Guilton was one of the richest of all known Jutish cemeteries. There, in at least two graves, were buried magnificent jewelled gold circular brooches of a kind found only in east Kent, and dating from soon after 600. In others, besides swords, some with ornate hilts, and other weapons, were glass bowls, pottery and jewellery. One Guilton grave contained a coin of Justinian so could not be earlier than his reign (527-65), and presumably none was later than 742 when burial outside a churchyard was forbidden. Yet at least 16 graves produced Roman objects, including three glass mirrors of 1st-century workmanship: either these were treasured possessions handed down as heirlooms for several generations before being buried with their last owners, or the Jutish cemetery lies above a Roman (or earlier pagan Anglo-Saxon) one. Faussett himself believed that there were many Roman cremation-burials there, beneath the Jutish burials.

There have been other casual finds in the area, including an important sixth-century pagan warrior cremation-burial in a bronze bowl at Coombe found about 1845, and a silver-gilt square-headed brooch of around 600, found many years ago at Cop Street or Goldstone, and closely matching another found in a grave at Guilton.

More finds have been made at Guilton over many years. A jewelled gold disc brooch was found as recently as 1973. Most notably, in 1957 there was concern among archaeologists when a sword and two green glass vases were dug up close to the mill after they had been located by a 'dowser', Major Pogson (who had previously used his skills to help find 'treasure' in the Tower of London). The Ministry of Works intervened, and listed the site as an ancient monument, to stop further digging. The full extent of the cemetery may not yet have been identified.

10 An Anglo-Saxon urn, of yellow-green glass corded with raised spiral lines, of *c*.600, found at Guilton in the 1950s (photograph by J.D. Ogilvie).

* * * *

In 596 Pope Gregory sent Augustine, prior of St Andrew's in Rome, as head of a mission to convert the heathen English to Christianity. After a false start when, hearing how fierce the English were, Augustine's courage failed and he returned to Rome, he and 40 monks set out again. In the spring of 597 they landed in Kent.

> At that time Aethelbehrt, King of Kent, was a very powerful monarch ... Beside the eastern parts of Kent there is a large island called Thanet ... divided from the mainland by the river Wantsum, which is about three furlongs wide, can be crossed in two places only, and joins the sea at either end. Here Augustine, the servant of the Lord, landed with his companions ... Augustine sent to Aethelbehrt, to say that he had come from Rome bearing the best of news ... On hearing this, the King ordered them to remain on the island where they had landed, and be provided with all things necessary, until he had decided what to do ... (Some knowledge of the Christian religion had already reached him, because he had a Christian wife, of the Frankish royal family, whose name was Bertha) ...
>
> Some days afterwards, the King came to the island and, sitting in the open air, commanded Augustine and his comrades to come there to talk to him. He took care that they should not meet in a building, for he held the traditional superstition that, if they practised magic, they might deceive and get the better of him as soon as he went inside. But they came endowed with divine, not devilish, power; and bearing as their standard a silver cross, and the image of our Lord and Saviour painted on a panel. They chanted litanies and uttered prayers to the Lord for their own eternal salvation, and the salvation of those to whom they had come. At the King's command, they sat down and preached the Word of Life ...
>
> Then he said, 'The words and promises you bring are fair enough. Because they are new to us and doubtful, I cannot agree to accept them and give up those beliefs which I and the whole English race have held so long. But you have come on a long pilgrimage; and I see you want to share with us things which you believe to be true and good. We do not wish to do you harm ... Nor do we forbid you to win all you can to your faith and religion, by your preaching.' So he gave them a dwelling in the city of Canterbury, which was the chief city of all his dominions ...

Written by Bede about 730, this suggests that it was on the Thanet shore of the Wantsum that Augustine landed, perhaps at Ebbsfleet, the site which has become traditional. But at Richborough the walls of the Roman Saxon Shore fort, then higher and more complete than today—the east wall did not fall until about 1560—would have provided a secure shelter for the open-air meeting. William Boys, in his history of Sandwich, quoted from manuscripts where it was written that Ethelbert was told that Augustine

> ... was come from Rome to bring unto him and his people the glad tidinge of the gospell, the way unto eternall life and blisse to all them that believe the same; which thing the King hearinge, came shortly after into the isle of Thanet unto his pallace or castle of Rupticester, or Richeborow, scituate nigh the old citty of Stonehore, and the King, sitting under the cliff or rock whereon the castle is built, commanded Augustine with his fellows to be brought before him.

Certainly some time before 1000 a chapel, dedicated to St Augustine, was built actually within the walls of Richborough Castle. In it was preserved a stone, said to be that on which Augustine had first stepped ashore in England, on which the impression of his foot had been miraculously left. For centuries before the Reformation, pilgrims flocked there on the anniversary of the landing, to pray for their health to be restored.

* * * *

The Romans' name for Richborough, *Ritupis*, was probably British—'on the ford': it became *Reptacaestir* (by 730), then *Raette* (about 1090), *Ratteburg* (1197), *Retesbrough* (14th-century) and, finally, *Richborowe* (1509). The river name Stour is also probably British (*Stur*, 686—'strong, powerful stream'. Names the later settlers gave to their villages and homesteads show that the broad pattern of the east Kent countryside was created long before the Norman conquest. Some of the earliest to be written down included Minster (*Menstre*, in a grant of land of 694), on the north bank of the river Stour; Wingham (*Uuingincggaham*, 834—'Wiga's people's village'), which included all of what is now Ash parish; Sandwich (*Sandwic*, 850); and Preston (*Preostantun*, 941—'the priests' village'), north-west of Ash. King Cenwulf of Mercia gave Wingham and '*Scealdeforda*' ('the shallow ford', somewhere west of Eastry and east and north of Wingham) to Archbishop Wilfred in 821. ('*Scealdeforda*' was also mentioned in 834, but never again.)

Other places existing before the Conquest included Fleet (*Fletes*, 'creek') in Ash parish, Each (*Ece*, 'oak-tree'), Woodnesborough (*Waneberge*, 'Woden's hill'), and Marshborough (*Masseberge*, '"Spotty's" hill') (the three last adjoining Ash parish to the south-east, and all four mentioned in Domesday, 1086); Goldstone (*Goldestanestune*, 1086, 'Goldstan's homestead'), Goss Hall (*Gosehal*', 1086, '(wild) goose hollow') both in Ash parish; and Stourmouth (*Sturemude*), Walmestone (at the western edge of Ash parish) (*Wielmeston*, 'Wighelm's homestead'), and Ash itself (*Aesce*, 'ash-tree'), all three included in a survey of the archbishops' estates of about 1093).

Beginning in 835, Ash, in common with much of east Kent, suffered intermittently for more than 200 years from a new threat from the sea. In 30 years there were more than a dozen raids by the Danes on England; in 850 a Danish army wintered on Thanet; in the following year 350 ships' companies stormed Canterbury, and in 854—in the first naval battle in recorded English history—a Danish fleet was defeated off Sandwich. Much later, in the summer of 1006, the Danes occupied Sandwich and raided the surrounding countryside; and in 1009 the people of Canterbury and east Kent were forced to buy off, with a 'gift' of £3,000, the most formidable Danish fleet to visit England for many years. In 1011 Canterbury was besieged and betrayed to the Danes, who captured and murdered Archbishop Aelfheah; and in 1013 Sweyn the Dane twice came to Sandwich. After peace between 1016 and 1042 while Cnut reigned over both England and Denmark, a Danish force plundered Sandwich in 1048. For some time Edward the Confessor concentrated a great fleet at Sandwich. In May 1066, after Edward's death, Tostig, brother of the new king Harold, occupied the town, carrying off local seamen when he left.

Four

The Normans at Ash and the Rise of Sandwich

In October 1066 William of Normandy landed in England. After the Battle of Hastings, fought on Saturday 14 October, William set out for London by way of Dover, where he spent eight days fortifying the town before moving to Canterbury, where he stayed a month. The story of William's expedition to England is displayed on the Bayeux Tapestry, perhaps commissioned by Bishop Odo of Bayeux, William's half-brother, and embroidered at Canterbury. It shows one of Odo's tenants, Vital, as a mounted knight bringing news to William before the battle. The inscription reads 'HIC : VVILLELM : DUX INTERROGAT : VITAL : SI VIDISSET EXERCITV HAROLDI' [Here Duke William asks Vital if he has seen Harold's army.] Vital was rewarded with estates in east Kent, at Canterbury, Whitstable and Preston, and also at Walmestone, part of the manor of Wingham.

The manor of Wingham, granted after 834 to successive archbishops by the English kings, included the present parishes of Wingham, Ash, Goodnestone and Nonington, and parts of Staple and Womenswold. So, both in Domesday Book and in the survey of Archbishop Lanfranc's estates of about 1093, his lands in Ash were listed under Wingham.

11   Vital of Walmstone, 1066, depicted on the Bayeux Tapestry, which was probably embroidered at Canterbury, where Vital also owned property, in 1066-77.

12 Wingham Barton: the 16th-century house built on what had been the demesne land of the archbishops' manor.

On the manor lived 85 villeins (mostly peasant farmers) and 20 bordars (probably cottagers) who worked 57 plough teams, and eight serfs. There were two water-mills, woodland enough to be assessed to pay five pigs annually, as well as two small woods producing fencing. It was all worth £100 a year. Barton—'Wingham Barton'—formed an important part of the archbishops' demesne (i.e. their home farm), on which there were eight plough teams. Five men then held substantial estates from the Archbishop, valued at £21 a year: Arnold at Goshall and Goldstone; Wibert at Knell; Herengod at Overland, all in what is now Ash parish; and Vital of Canterbury at Walmestone, on the western edge of Ash. (The estate of the fifth man, Godfrey 'the bowman', was at Ratling in Nonington.) Between them, they had eight plough teams. On their land lived 22 bordars and eight serfs.

Also in Ash, at Fleet, the Norman lord of Folkestone William of Arques held, as part of the manor of Wingham, an estate probably held from him by Roger and Osbert, 'the butlers', where there were 'on the demesne one plough-team and four villeins', and 'a knight with one plough team', all worth 40s. There, on the shore of the Wantsum, was a fishery (probably a weir with netting and fencing) with a saltpan, making salt (necessary to preserve meat for winter consumption) by evaporation from sea-water, valued at 30d. a year.

There were then churches at Ash and at Walmestone (probably actually at Over-land), two of the six daughter-churches of Wingham—which paid the archbishops annually 2s. at Easter, and also a 'sestar' of honey, eight lambs, and 60 loaves, and 12d. for wine and 14d. for oil, and to the Papal See 14s. 4d. in Romescot ('Peter's Pence')—as well as another at Fleet, one of ten subordinate to Folkestone church. There was also a separate church at 'Raette', perhaps inside the walls of Richborough Castle, which paid the archbishops 7d. annually at Easter.

In 1084 or 1085 Archbishop Lanfranc founded the Priory of St Gregory at Canterbury, one of the first houses of canons regular to adopt the Augustinian order, the Austin Canons. In its original endowment he included the tithes of Arnold's lordships of Goshall and Goldstone, and of Osbern's lordship of Fleet. In the early 13th century Adam of Sissinghurst purchased, and then gave to the Priory, a rentcharge on land at Overland; Hugh of Goshall gave it two acres of land at Goldstone on which its grange later stood, his son Robert of Goshall gave it an adjoining three acres, and Thomas, son of Hugh the Butler of Fleet, gave it 50 acres in the Fleet marshes (from which 4s. a year had to be paid to compound for all services except that of making a sea-wall). (At the Dissolution, 450 years later, the Priory's estates were exchanged by the king with the archbishop, became part of the revenues of the see of Canterbury, were let on long leases, and were not split up until the death of George Gipps, the last lessee, in 1800.)

It may be possible to identify these individual 11th-century landholdings more precisely. The separate tithe districts in Ash, preserved until 1840, certainly derive from very early estate boundaries, and otherwise unexplained steep banks may also do so.

The Manor of Wingham.

THE COURT BARON of SIR HENRY CHUDLEIGH OXENDEN BART., Lord of the said Manor of Wingham, will be holden at the RED LION INN, in WINGHAM, on THURSDAY, the Twentieth Instant, at Twelve o'clock at noon; at which time and place all Persons who owe suit and service to the said Court Baron are hereby required to make their personal appearance to perform the same, to pay up all their Arrears of Quit Rents, Copy Rents, and Reliefs, and to enter their Estates held of the said Manor with proper Descriptions on the Court Rolls, according to the ancient usage and customs of the said Manor; otherwise they will be proceeded against for their default.

WIGHTWICK, KINGSFORD, and FRASER,
Stewards.

Canterbury, 7th November 1862.

---

13   Public Notice of Court Baron of Wingham Manor from the *Kent Herald*, 13 November 1862; the archbishops' manor had passed into lay hands at the Reformation.

With the Norman conquest came comparative peace for east Kent. Conflicts became largely ones of warring personalities within the kingdom. Part of the struggle between Henry II and his archbishop Thomas Becket was played out here. In November 1170 Becket infuriated the King by excommunicating the Archbishop of York and two other bishops. He avoided royal officials waiting at Dover to seize him as he returned to England on 1 December, by landing instead at Sandwich. His 12-mile journey to Canterbury, through Ash and Wingham, took the whole day.

> All the way to Canterbury the roads were lined with praying and rejoicing multitudes; it was like a triumphal procession ... Wherever the Archbishop passed, a swarm of poor folk, small and great, young and old, flocked to meet him, some prostrating themselves in the way before him, others tearing off their garments and strewing them in the way, crying aloud, again and again, 'Blessed is he that cometh in the name of the Lord.

On 29 December Becket was murdered on the altar steps of his cathedral. Henry II himself died in July 1189. His successor, his son Richard 'Coeur de Lion', spent only six months in England in his 10-year reign. On his second visit he landed at Sandwich on 13 March 1194, after spending nearly two years imprisoned in Austria. He is said to have walked the whole way to Canterbury, to return thanks at Becket's tomb for his release. (He sailed again from Portsmouth on 17 April, never to return.)

Richard's successor, his brother John, held his Court at the archbishops' manor at Wingham in May 1213, while expecting an invasion from France. On 20 May 1216, Louis, Dauphin of France, landed at Stonar with an army to claim the English throne. Watched by John, who dared not challenge him, Louis sacked the town of Sandwich. John's death brought only a short truce; on 29 April 1217 Louis landed again, and burnt Sandwich. The new king of England, Henry III, was only nine years old. The bishops and barons rallied to him and, on St Bartholomew's Day, 24 August 1217, the Cinque Ports' fleet put out from Sandwich and defeated the French. William, Earl Marshal and Regent, decided some of the spoils should be used to found a hospital at Sandwich in honour of St Bartholomew, 'who on that day had given them the victory'.

By 1252 there were Wednesday markets at Canterbury and Sandwich. In that year, the king granted Archbishop Boniface the right to hold a Tuesday market at Wingham, the Hundred Court jury having found that neighbouring markets would be improved by traders coming also to Wingham. (But in 1290 it was said that the Wingham market had injured the Canterbury market; that it intercepted goods on the road, and drove up their price in Canterbury.) In 1255 a 10-year-old elephant, a present from the king of France to Henry III, was landed at Sandwich, and taken to the Tower of London.

In the Barons' War between 1258 and 1267, Sandwich supported Simon de Montfort against Henry III, but de Montfort was killed at Evesham in August 1265. Early in January 1266, the Lord Edward, Henry's son, with Roger de Leybourne—Lord Warden of the Cinque Ports (and owner of estates at Overland and elsewhere in Ash, as well as at Preston)—advanced through east Kent from Canterbury to Eastry, from where they attacked and captured Sandwich on 17 January. Edward sensibly followed this by a reconciliation with the Ports, restoring to them the trade on which they depended. As Sandwich grew in importance as a trading port, reaching a peak of prosperity in the 1260s, the surrounding countryside shared in its fortunes. In 1269 the river Thames was

14 Ash Level, gradually drained in medieval times as the Wantsum Channel was pushed back into what became the bed of the river Stour.

frozen 'from St Andrew's tide to Candlemas', so that merchandise from Sandwich had to be taken to London by land instead of by sea, and the road through Ash must have seen a busy winter.

More local place names began to appear: Elmstone (north-west of Ash parish) (*Elm' est'*, *c.*1175, 'Aegelmaer's homestead'); Hills Court, in Ash (*Hulles,* 1200, 'hills'); Staple (south of Ash) (*Stapl'*, 1205, 'standing stone(s)' (south of Ash parish); Knell (*Ulmis,* 1210, 'elm-trees'), Guilton (*Geldentun,* 1218, 'the golden homestead', i.e. probably, where yellow flowers grew, rather than where the 'golden idol' of tradition was to be found), Molland (*Molland,* 1226, 'estate for which a money rent is paid'), Overland (*Euerland,* 1226, 'estate on a ridge'), Ware (*War,* 1226, 'weir'), and Coombe (*Cumbe,* 1235, 'valley') (all in Ash); Shatterling (*Scat'ling,* 1240, 'the vagrants' settlement') (poor, sandy common land as recently as the beginning of the 19th century, lying west of Ash, on the boundaries of Ash, Staple and Wingham); Hoaden (*de Haddon,* 1240, 'heather down'), Rubery Drove (*de Runeberg,* 1240, 'rough hill'), Weddington (*Wedington,* 1251, 'Waedda's homestead'), Pedding (*de Pedinge,* 1251, 'the place of the fat fellow's people'), Barton *(de la Berton,* 1254, 'barley farm', 'the home farm'), and Corking (*Cocking,* 1278, 'the place of the big fellow's people'), all in Ash. Lowton (probably from *hlawtun,* 'homestead on the hill'), Wass (perhaps from *waesse,* 'wet place') and Westmarsh (perhaps originally *waesse mersc,* 'Wass marsh'), all in Ash, must date from about the same time.

FIVE

SEPARATION FROM WINGHAM, 1282

In 1282 the Welsh princes Llewellyn and David were in open rebellion againsr the English king, Edward I, and in April Archbishop John Peckham (a Franciscan, an Englishman, and perhaps a man of Kent, who had been appointed to the see of Canterbury in 1279) ordered their excommunication. By August the king was in North Wales with an army and 60 ships of the Cinque Ports fleet. The archbishop joined him there, and tried unsuccessfully to mediate between king and princes. (On 10 December Llewellyn was slain at Radnor; the following June David was betrayed, and executed.)

Before leaving for Wales Peckham spent some time in Kent, and at the end of June he was at his manor house at Wingham. While there, he put into effect a scheme, first proposed by his predecessor Robert Kilwardby, to divide the huge parish, the largest of the archbishops' Kent estates (first given to them by Athelstan, somehow lost in the troubled times which followed, and restored to them by Eadmund in 941), and to establish at Wingham a college of canons. The foundation deed was signed on 29 June.

BROTHER JOHN, by Divine Permission Archbishop of Canterbury, Primate of All England ... eternal greeting to all in the Lord. The providence of the Supreme Father, whose rule sets the boundaries of the whole creation, has entrusted His vineyard to keepers, and gives to each according to his own capacity and measure of grace, lest the magnitude of the entrusted talent should exceed the strength and diligence of the steward, so that the treasury of the Lord be diminished, the vineyards laid waste, and the flock ... owing to the inability of the earthly shepherd, be wasted by the wolf without hindrance. We therefore in our anxiety for the living fruit ... have turned our eyes to the church of Wingham as it were to a fruitful vineyard filled with branches and fruits, which cannot easily be cultivated by the labours of one husbandman ... from the great extent of the parish as well as its numerous population ... We have therefore divided it into four parishes ... The first and chief of all these we declare to be the church of Wingham together with all its hamlets and our archiepiscopal tithes of Berton together with the chapel and tithes of Overland and all its tenants; and with it all the tithes of Campi Crul. The second, the parish of Ash having the tithes which were given to Geldenton, together with the chapel of Flete and all its hamlets ... The third, the church of Goodnestone with its hamlets ... The fourth the church of Nonington, with the Chapel of Womenswold, and its hamlets ...

In the 13th century the demesne lands on the manor of Wingham, farmed by the archbishops' bailiff, included 29 acres in *Siredland*, 43¾ acres in *Torbestegh*, and 102½ acres in *Blakeney*. There were also 34½ acres '*apud la Med*', perhaps a piece lying on its own. A large part of the Wingham demesne lay in Ash parish, at *Berton*. The demesne mostly consisted of parts of large fields, the other parts of which were farmed by tenants. (Although the tenants' arable land lay next to demesne arable, there is no evidence that the strips of tenants' and demesne arable ever shared a common cropping rotation, as in the common field system characteristic of some parts of England. Certainly by the 15th century the Wingham demesne was cropped separately.)

The archbishops' requirements of their unfree tenants were of two kinds: help with cultivating the demesne land, and 'boon work'. After harvest, when the stubble was grazed, those tenants whose lands lay next to demesne land could not prevent their beasts, including draught oxen going to plough, from grazing demesne stubble as well as their own, so the archbishops' bailiff demanded in return a general ploughing service. One acre of ploughing, sowing and harrowing ('*gavelerth*') was required from each tenant who had a fully yoked plough, proportionately less from those with less. If a tenant joined with someone who was not himself a tenant of the manor to make up a full team for his own ploughing, he was also obliged to do his plough service on the demesne with a full team. The archbishops' bailiff made up composite plough teams for the day's work on the demesne from the various tenants' oxen, and put any odd beast left over to draw a harrow. Ploughmen had the right to a meal at the archbishops' expense when they worked on the demesne. However, from about 5,500 acres on the Wingham manor which owed it, the whole gavel ploughing only covered about 30 acres out of 1,200 acres of demesne arable. Although reaping service ('*gavelrip*') was demanded at twice that rate, these labour services were not a heavy burden. Boon work, to meet urgent needs on the demesne, which also carried a daily food allowance (said at Wingham to be worth 3d. for every plough), was probably not done by the tenant personally, but by his hired men. But, more tiresomely, tenants were also required to help supply, carry and store provisions needed during the archbishops' visits to Wingham—or, more often, to Canterbury. This duty ('*averagium*') began as soon as an archbishop's arrival was announced, and lasted as long as he stayed. At Wingham his steward summoned as many men as he wanted; and they were expected to take their turn, and to stay all day. A tenant could find a substitute, but if he defaulted altogether he was liable to a fine, as well as to pay for the extra work which the archbishop's own servants had had to do. Tenants were also liable to supply hay and litter for the archbishop's retinue. Archbishop Stephen Langton's steward had been notoriously strict, and was long remembered for cutting down the food allowances to the Wingham manor tenants when they performed this carrying service. It became increasingly irksome: in 1390 Archbishop Courtenay summoned to appear before him at his castle at Saltwood six men who had failed to do it, and sentenced them to parade round Wingham church like penitents, 'walking with slow steps, and each carrying on his shoulders a sack of hay and straw'.

Besides cultivating the arable lands, the archbishops' bailiffs were beginning to drain the Ash Level, as were the monks of the Cathedral priory on their manor of Monkton on the other shore of the Wantsum. By the 13th century, the Flemings' marsh ('*mariscus Flemingorum*') had been reclaimed. Perhaps in 'Corner Drove' there survives the name of the Canterbury monk, William de la Corner, who became Bishop of Sarum in 1289. But the archbishop's accounts for 1273-4 reveal a startlingly high mortality among

15   *Left.* The effigy is probably Sir John Leverick (d. *c*.1375). This etching of 1811 is by Charles Stothard, who had first to scrape thick layers of whitewash from the figure with his penknife.

16   *Above.* The effigies are probably Sir John de Goshall (d. *c*.1306) and, beneath him, his lady (d. *c*.1300). This etching of 1864 was taken from a photograph by William Dixon, the village chemist. Soon afterwards, the floor level of the chancel was raised, and the brasses were moved.

the grazing sheep: in that year 409 out of 545 sheep on the Wingham demesne died before shearing.

For 60 years before 1282, the largest estate in Ash, at Goss Hall and Goldstone, had been held from the archbishops by the Goshall family. Weddington probably still formed part of it, and the lands later known as Levericks were not sold to Henry Loverick until 1306. In 1282 the estate belonged to Henry de Goshall. Soon after-wards Ash church was rebuilt, all but its Norman west tower, very likely at the expense of the Goshall family, whose tombs they intended the chancel should contain. They were wealthy, and they lived in the parish. Margery de Goshall had to pay 50s. towards the Lay Subsidy in 1334, the second highest assessment in Kent. In 1366 Elizabeth de Gosehall, widow of Sir John, was licensed to hear mass in an oratory in her own house. Three years later, she gave houses and lands to support a chaplain in the church of Ash. On her death soon after 1379, the estate passed to her son-in-law Thomas St Nicholas. (A stone coffin, which may have been hers, was discovered at Goss Hall about 1709.)

In 1282, other lands at Goldstone, Knell and Overland belonged to the Leybourne family, held with their manor of Preston. Roger de Leybourne had died on crusade with Prince Edward in 1271. William de Leybourne, who held the estate in 1282, was 'Captain of the King's Mariners and Admiral of the English Seas'. His great-grand-daughter Juliana, Countess of Huntingdon, possessed a private chapel at Preston where 'divers vestments, books and other ornaments' were valued at £31 0s. 8d. at the time of her death in 1367.

17   St Nicholas Church, Ash. All but the tower dates from about 1282. The central crossing-tower was inserted about 1475, probably replacing an earlier, lower, central tower.

At Fleet, Robert de Vere, 5th Earl of Oxford, held an estate from John de Sandwich who in turn held from the archbishop. It had been in the de Vere family since 1208, and remained so until the reign of Elizabeth I. Other land at Fleet was held, as part of the archbishops' manor of Wingham, by John le Boteler, whose family had been related to Archbishop Hubert Walter. In 1197 an estate at Fleet, reckoned as half a knight's fee, had consisted of 'a capital messuage within the walls of Richborough Castle', fields known as '*Cnolla, Claure, Hoga, Nallis, Scantega, Staldingburg, Pasture,* and *Stepatra*', fields 'north of *Hoga*', 'south of the thorn-bushes', 'north of the road running to the walls of Richborough', and 'south of the wall of Richborough', one acre 'outside the walls of the western gate in the wall', and one acre 'south of the Lady Isobel's houses', as well as 'marshes and saltpans'. It was partitioned then, and Estrilda wife of Wifi, Luke and Philip, sons of Wifi, Nicholas son of Wimund (for 10 acres only), Jordan de Fleet (except for half his 'cart-service'), and Edric de Sauner, were thenceforth to be tenants of Elias de Beauchamp and his wife Constance Bolebec. Roland d'Avranches was to have the 'messuage in the field south of the thorn-bushes, and the ground where the thorn-bushes are … next to the mill', and Alan of Bereling, Albrea wife of Godwin, William the Scot, Humphrey and Roger, sons of Wlwin, Nicholas, son of Wimund (for five acres), Matthew son of Osbert, were to be his tenants. The marshes and saltpans, and the services and rents due from Roger Bulege and Walter Hazard, were to be shared equally. Elias de Beauchamp and his wife were to have 3½d. of the rent due from Alice d'Anjou, and 3¾d. of that due from Edric son of Richard. Roland d'Avranches was to have the other 2½d. due from Alice, and the other 1¾d. and two hens due from Edric.

In 1296, on the 5th Earl's death, his manor of Flete, held by service of one knight's fee, and worth £30 19s. 5½d. per annum, included 'a capital messuage with its curtilage, dovecote and certain closes' worth 6s. 8d., 80 acres of arable worth 2s. an acre, 315 acres of marshland worth 1s. an acre, and money rents totalling £6 7s. 5d. at 'Michaelmas, the Feast of St Martin and at the Feast of the Purification', and 27 cocks worth 1½d. each and 42 hens worth 2d. each at 'the Nativity of Our Lord'.

In 1282, Hills Court belonged to Thomas de Helles, descended from Theodore de Helles and Agnes, sister of Becket. He died in 1288. Sir Henry de Helles was a knight of the shire for Kent in 1331, and Gilbert de Helles of Hills Court the sheriff of Kent in 1356.

It is not certain who else owned land in Ash in 1282. Andrew de Molland had sold property to Thomas de Sandwich in 1271. When Thomas' son, Sir Nicholas de Sandwich, died about 1350, Molland passed to his son-in-law, John Septvans, in whose family it was to remain until 1695. By 1303 Chequer perhaps belonged to Ralph 'de Chekker'. In 1337 Roger de Estcheker was appointed 'to keep watch and ward in that part of the coast of Kent between Sandwich and Reculver', i.e. along the Wantsum. John de Pedding was living here in 1279. William de Chilton died in 1303, and by 1331 Chilton had passed to William de Baude.

In 1285 the Statute of Winchester required 200 feet to be cleared on each side of roads linking market towns. In 1290 Edward I acquired the rights of the Priory of Christchurch at Canterbury over the port of Sandwich, and in 1293 he also acquired Hull, and renamed it Kingston-on-Hull. At both places he took steps to provide good approaches by land. It was probably then that the 'causeway' across the marsh between Sandwich and Each was completed. The king himself landed at Sandwich on 14 March 1298, on his return from France.

It was still a violent society. On 14 August 1300, three royal justices (including Ralph de Sandwich) were on their way to Sandwich with an armed guard, probably to scrutinise the claim by Sandwich and the other Cinque Ports to be exempt from the jurisdiction of the royal courts and to a privileged tax position, in return for the naval and other services which the Ports rendered to the king. When they reached Ash they were set upon. More than 25 Sandwich townsmen, including the mayor and town clerk, did

> assault the aforesaid justices of the king with force and arms … and ill-treat them, not permitting them to enter the king's town of Sandwich or to do the duty enjoined on them by the king, and cut open the pouch with the king's rolls, and break the bows and arrows of the men of the aforesaid justices, and inflict other outrages upon them, in contempt of the king and the obvious hurt of the royal crown and dignity.

To justify this attack, the men of Sandwich straight away drew up a custumal, setting out the liberties they claimed.

The king's judges who visited Kent in 1313 heard five cases from Ash of violent death and crime. Robert, son of Nicholas Wood of Chilton, playing with other boys in his father's meadow, had fallen into a pond and drowned. While driving a cart drawn by four horses, Nicholas Wood himself had been knocked down and dragged across a field, so that he too had died: verdict, misadventure; but the value of the horses and cart (54s. 10d.), the cause of the tragedy, to be forfeit to the sheriff, as a 'deodand'. Joanna, wife of William Lefevre atte Hill, and her daughter Isabella, had broken into John de Gosehall's house by night, carted away his goods, and fled. William de Oxteghe, Thomas son of Otho de Updowne, Osbert Coppe and Agnes Lehe (daughter of William Coppe) had all come by night to Christina Harlewyne's house in Chilton, and had there so beaten and wounded a cleric, Robert de Whytefeld, that he died: verdict, murder; and their lands and goods to be forfeit. Unable to enter John White's house at Chilton by the door, another cleric, John Bunter, had broken a window to get in. When White arrived home they had quarrelled, and Bunter had been killed. White had fled, but was caught and lodged in Maidstone gaol. When he appeared before the Court he produced a pardon from the late king, Edward I, given to him in gaol, because he had killed Bunter in self-defence.

Six

Before the Reformation

In the 14th century, more names of places in the parish appeared. Some were manorial names: Guston (*de Guston*, 1332), Chequer (*Lescheker*, 1346); some were named from those who lived in them: Cop Street (*de Cobbestrete,* 1366, probably from William Cobbe, *fl.*1348), Levericks (from Henry Loverick, *fl.*1306), Cooper Street (*Cowper strete*, 1471 from John Cuppre, *fl.*1323), Paramour Street (1526, from William Paramor, *fl.*1327); and some from their situation: East Street (1483), Uphousden (*Ophosen*, 1484, 'the houses high up'), Barding Street, 'road in the valley where barley grows' (but Chapman Street and Harmon Street were also names for the same place). Durlock (1616) may come from *deorloca*, a former 'deer enclosure'.

During the Hundred Years' War, the parish must have been caught up by events in Sandwich. In 1342 Edward III waited several weeks in the town for the return from Brittany of troops held up by adverse winds, before marching to Portsmouth. In 1347, following the successful siege of Calais, after which the six burghers had been saved from hanging by Queen Phillipa's pleading, Edward landed at Sandwich with the Queen, their son Edward, the Black Prince, and their new-born daughter. To intercept a Spanish fleet, a squadron of 50 ships assembled at Sandwich in August 1350, manned by the flower of England's chivalry, among them nearly all the original knights of the Garter. In the spring of 1357, after the capture of the French king John at Poitiers, the Black Prince sailed from Bordeaux with his royal captive. After a tedious voyage they arrived at Sandwich, and 'took up their quarters in the town and neighbourhood' for two days, to refresh themselves before going on to Canterbury and London. In 1359 Edward III collected a great army with food and stores in more than 6,000 waggons and carts; it sailed from Sandwich for Calais in 1,100 ships.

In 1364 William, Lord Latimer, owner of the estate at Fleet formerly belonging to the Botelers, obtained a royal licence to hold a Thursday market at Ash, and an annual fair at Lady Day. The following year a great inundation destroyed Stonar and endangered 'the marches towards Canterbury'. Most Mediterranean goods bound for London were now transhipped at Sandwich, in 1377 the wool staple was transferred from Queenborough, and trade through Calais grew. For both Sandwich and Ash it was a prosperous as well as a troubled time. It was very likely Sandwich merchants who built or rebuilt houses in Ash: Molland, Chequer, Knell (since gone), The Mote at Hoaden (gone), Uphousden, Paramour, Goldstone, Weddington, Goshall, Richborough, Moat Farmhouse, and Pedding—conveniently close to, but safely outside, the unhealthily crowded town.

When followers of Wat Tyler set out in June 1381 to raise support in the villages of east Kent for the Peasants' Revolt, they may well have had little success in Ash, because John de Septvans of Chequer was first cousin to the Sheriff of Kent, Sir William de Septvans, whom they had assaulted and imprisoned at Canterbury.

In September 1397 Archbishop Thomas Arundel was impeached by Parliament, and sentenced to perpetual banishment. A survey of his Barton at Wingham found that it included 140 acres of arable land worth 12d. an acre yearly, 960 acres of marshland worth (over and above payments for 'the sea-wall') 6d. an acre, a windmill 'which used to pay 10 quarters of barley worth 3s. 4d. a quarter [equal to 8 bushels], but is worth nothing this year because the post is broken so that it cannot be used', and £1 11s. 9d. in yearly rents; a total of £32 11s. 9d. a year. On the Barton on 25 September there had been 4 horses worth 13s. 4d. each, 516 ewes and rams worth 12d. each, 106 lambs worth 8d. each, 68 quarters of wheat worth 5s. a quarter, 75 quarters of barley worth 3s. 4d. a quarter, 6 quarters of oats worth 20d. a quarter, 20 quarters of peas and 24 quarters of vetch worth 3s. 4d. a quarter, a cart with unshod wheels with harness for three horses worth 8s., four sets of plough-ropes with side-harness worth 4d., and 456 lb. of wool worth 2d. a pound, a total of £73 11s. 0d.

By the end of the 14th century a general economic decline, partly due to the fall in population caused by the Black Death, showed in the administration of the arch-bishops' estates. Archbishop Courtenay leased out at least 18 demesne farms. By 1422 most of them, though not Wingham, had been leased; and by 1450 Wingham followed. Archbishop Thomas Bourchier leased to William Peny, for 10 years from Michaelmas 1479, at a yearly rent of £25, 'the Manor of Barton Wingham' (previously let to Roger Colarde), including two arable fields called Westfeld and Herdeland, a meadow called 'le Haymede … lying between the marshes of the manors of Preston Elmestone and le Cornedrove wall on the west and the ditch called le Swynning leading from the common road as far as le Middelgates on the east', a weir, and 'the barn called le Westbarne with free coming and going to the same from the Estfield', with 'all other lands, marshes, rents, etc.'. Archbishop John Morton leased to Simon Gason and Thomas Pamor, also for 10 years at a yearly rent of £25, 'from the Feast of St Nicholas' (6 December) 1492 a barn within the manor of Barton Wingham called the Westbarne with free access to the same, an arable field called Estefelde, marshes called Bokyn lese, Eastmarsh and Newmarsh, and a saltpit 'in the saltmarsh opposite the aforesaid marsh'.

The Ash estates of the Leybournes passed by marriage to the Clinton family, and then to Richard Clitherow of Goldstone, Sheriff of Kent in 1403 and 'Admiral of the Seas from the Thames westwards' from 1405. In 1416 Henry V, recently victorious at Agincourt—where Richard's son Roger fought—sailed back to Calais from Sandwich. Less happily, the French landed at Sandwich in 1437 and plundered the town.

In July 1449 Roger Clitherow was 'violently expelled' from the manor of Knell by John Clinton of Ash who, with the help of Stephen Slegge the sheriff, carried away by force animals and goods worth £119 5s. 4d. The Kentish rising under Jack Cade in June 1450 was directed partly against Slegge's extortions, and among those pardoned for their part in it were several men from Sandwich, the Constables of the Hundreds of Preston and Wingham (in which Ash lay) 'and all and singular the men of the said Hundreds', as well as John Septvans, Esquire of the Body to Henry VI (whose effigy lies in Ash

18 *Left*. Maud (d.1440), daughter of Sir John Oldcastle, the Lollard burned at the stake 1417, and widow of Richard Clitherow of Goldstone, Sheriff of Kent 1402, Admiral of the Seas from the Thames westward 1405.

19 *Above*. Jane (d.1455), granddaughter of Richard Clitherow, wife of John Keriel, and sister-in-law of Sir Thomas Keriel, KG. Her horned head-dress is unique on a brass.

church). After an appeal to the royal judges, Knell was restored to Clitherow in August 1450.

Roger's daughter Jane (whose brass is also in Ash church) had married John Keriel of Westenhanger, who spent 22 years in French captivity after being taken prisoner in 1450—probably at the battle of Formigny near Bayeux, where the English commander was his elder brother, Sir Thomas Keriel, K.G. By this defeat—caused by English reliance on the longbow, which had won Agincourt, but was now outdated—Normandy was finally lost. But when in August 1457 an expedition from Harfleur landed 1,800 men near Sandwich to attack the town, it was Keriel who led the relieving force raised from the countryside around. The fighting went on for ten hours before the French withdrew, but only after pillaging the town and killing the mayor.

Several of the early incidents of the Wars of the Roses occurred in Sandwich, as rival armies successively occupied the town, marching to and from London. But it was at St Albans in February 1461 that Keriel, while acting as the bodyguard of the weak-minded Henry VI, was captured with the King by the Queen, Margaret of Anjou. Despite the King's entreaties, she had Keriel immediately beheaded in front of him.

Sandwich was 'newly walled, ditched and fortified' in the 1470s, and there belonged to the port 95 ships and over 1,500 seamen, but already the Wantsum was becoming difficult to navigate. In 1467 the Archbishop and the Abbot of St Augustine's were ordered to remove their weirs, groynes and kiddle-nets 'from the King's river, from Sandwich Haven to North Mouth'. Later, 'a caryke that was sonke in the haven in Pope Paulus' time' was locally believed to have been the original cause of the silting. Morton, archbishop between 1486 and 1500, was the first to take advantage of the receding waters by enclosing the saltings with seawalls. In 1523 Robert Toke's lease of the manor of Barton Wingham, for 15 years from Michaelmas 1523 at a yearly rent of £50, mentioned 'le Muddewall' as well as sheep-folds in the marsh, and required the archbishop to maintain the sewers within the marsh and the drains and dykes 'without' it.

20 The medieval parish chest in St Nicholas Church, from a woodcut by Adelaide Godfrey, 1864.

Pray for the soulys of Wyllm lewys & anys hyf Wyf thy dyed the xxiij day of martiuf in the yere of oW lord god M ccccc xxvj

21 The small, simple brass to William Leweis (d.1526), churchwarden of Overland, and his wife Anys, was probably made locally at Canterbury.

The lease included 13 acres in Eastfield ('bounded by land of William Lewes towards the west, by land called Carpenters towards the east, by the aforesaid manor towards the north, by land of Simon Gason and the land of Overland Chapel towards the south'), 74 acres in Westfeld ('bounded by land called Hadmersshe Elmestone and Preston towards the west, by the aforesaid manor towards the east, by land of Simon Gason and John Peny towards the south, and by the marsh called Cowlese towards the north'), 66 acres in the field called Warehawthorne ('bounded by land of Richard Creke towards the east, by land of Simon Gason and others towards the west, by the land called Bullocklese towards the north, and by the king's highway from Ware to Goldston towards the south'), and the whole of the marsh called Westmarsh ('bounded by the stream towards the north, by land of the Manor of Goldstone and the land of the Chantry of Asshe towards the east, by land of the Lordship of the Manor towards the south, and by the marshes of Elmeston and Preston towards the west'). The lease also included 300 of the archbishop's ewes (at 16d. each).

In medieval England, a wealthy man often provided in his will for a priest to sing masses after his death and on its anniversary, for the repose of his soul and those of all the faithful departed. This endowment, to provide a stipend for the priest, was known as a chantry. In 1403 Gilbert Aflete, Henry Peny and John atte Stile of Nelle, were licensed by Archbishop Arundel to settle two messuages, 40 acres of land and 72 acres of marsh at Ash, part of the archbishop's manor of Wingham, to endow a Chantry of St Mary, to enable 'a priest to celebrate divine service, for the wholesome estate of the said persons while they lived and for their souls when they were dead, and for certain other persons and for their friends and benefactors and all Christian souls, every day in the parish church of Ash.'

A second chantry at Ash, the Chantry of the Upper Hall or Septvans Chantry, was founded about 1450 by John Septvans, so that a priest might celebrate masses for his soul and all Christian souls for ever. He endowed the chantry with a farm at St Nicholas in Thanet. John Septvans died in 1458, and his widow, Katherine Martyn of Faversham, in 1498. She and Henry and Alice Downing all gave property in Ash to augment the chantry's endowment.

Gifts in the wills of Ash parishioners show their widespread concern about the state of the parish roads. In 1481 Edward Fanting left 'To the repair of various bad roads in the parish; viz. Armyntstreet, Thornthy, Trippistreet, and the road between the vicarage and the church, 10 marks'; in 1526 William Lewies left 'To the highway between Nasshe and Culmer 40s., and between Eche and Sandwich 20s.'; and in 1554 John Rafe 'to mending the highway between Gilden town and Ash church where most needed 20s.'

Other gifts suggest heavy expenditure between 1475 and 1502 on 'church works' at Ash. About that time the central crossing-tower was built, to replace the old Norman tower in the north-west corner (possibly destroyed or damaged in the great earthquake of 1382), and probably encasing the piers of an earlier, lower crossing-tower of about 1285. There were many bequests towards the maintenance of the high altar, and gifts to the Chancel of Our Lady and the Chapel of St Thomas the Martyr and to their altars, to altars of St John Baptist, of St Katherine and of the Trinity, to the tabernacle of the Image of Our Lady in Our Lady's choir, and to the Images of St Mary Magdalene, St Nicholas and St John Baptist. Each altar had its light, and each place in the parish had its own: the lights of Hoden, of Nell, of Fleet, of Ash Street, 'called Barding', 'of the brodered of Nash', and the 'Light of the Street called Hoc light'. There were gifts of service-books: 'one missal', 'for a Porifer', 'for one Antiphoner or other book', 'one processional'; and for furnishings: a cross cloth, a herse cloth, and a canopy for the sacrament. Richard a Beere left 20s. in 1514 'for a new paire of organs'. William Creke gave 2 marks in 1518 and William Lewies 10 marks in 1526 'to the gilding of the Rood Loft'.

Many wills included a wish to be buried in the churchyard. In 1486 William Norreys of Brokes (now Moat Farm) gave directions that his body should be 'buried in the chancel of Our Lady in the parish church of Ash, at the south end of the altar there', that

> my red cloth of Baudekyn be laid upon my body in Ash church, and there remain for a perpetual remembrance and especially to be prayed for there; with a herse and black cloth with two tapers thereupon set, to be alight and burning the time of saying divine service there, to be ordained and had over my tomb for a special remembrance of prayer;

and that 'a convenient stone be set in the wall afore my tomb under the image of Mary Magdalene there, with an image of the Holy Trinity graven in brass, and piktures of my body and arms therein set.'

In 1498 Katherine Martyn desired to be 'buried in the parish church of St Nicholas of Ash, in the same tomb where the body of John Septvans formerly my husband, resteth'. William Lewies, who died in 1526, expressed the wish to be 'buried in the church of St Nicholas before the altar of St John the Baptist there', and directed 'that there be a stone to lye on my grave with the pykture of me and my wife upon the said stone'. (Katherine Martyn's alabaster effigy, alongside her first husband's, and the brass 'pykture' of Lewies and his wife may still be seen in the church, but William Norreys' tomb is lost.)

Lewies was one of the churchwardens of Overland chapel in 1511. In 1513, Thomas Brige left 'to the Light of Our Lady in the chapel at Ov'land one bushel of barley and the light of St Stephen in the same chapel a bushel of barley'.

22 John Septvans, Esquire of the Body to Henry VI (d.1458), nephew of Joan, wife of Sir John Leverick. The alabaster figure was almost certainly carved near Nottingham. His widow Katherine Martin (d.1498) lies next to him—and she can be seen in this photograph. They do not fit the tomb-chest here, on which they have lain since 1620 or earlier.

Many wills included bequests for the relief of the poor. Alice Downing, who died in 1511, left the poor all her 'body raiment' as well as 40s. 'in shirts smocks hoses and shoes'.

In a community closely tied to its land, with little ready money about, many Ash wills included gifts of grain or livestock. In 1459 Thomas Pomflett left his 'daughter Isabell two cows, 25 ewes and £13 6s. 8d., Agnes and Margaret Whitlok six ewes each, Robert Bregge one horse called Gryme, John Serlys a pig with two bushels of corn, Thomas Petite a young bullock.' When Henry Ford died in 1479 he said his wife Joan was to 'have a cow, 25 ewes, four quarters of grain, eight quarters of corn, and four pigs called Bakyn hoggs; to my daughter a mare, and to each of my children six ewes.' In 1484 John Broke of Brooke Street left to the 'high altar 12d. and six ewes, and to the work of the church six ewes', and provided for his 'wife Joan to have my best horse and cow; son John another horse and two calves; son Thomas a cow, son Henry one heifer', in 1487 William Perye said his two daughters Elyn and Annes should each have a bullock, and in 1513 Edmund Pratt left his wife Juliana 'three kine and all my household stuff; daughters Isabell and Alice each five ewes'. Much later, in 1556, John Reede, yeoman, left his wife Thomasin '£50, eight kine, two horses, 40 ewes, half my household stuff, and all my poultry', and declared that 'Thomas Hoole, my servant, shall have his sheep and lambs that be with me, and one quarter of barley'.

In his will made in 1485, John Carpenter of Westmarsh carefully described the land he owned: 'two and a half acres of land, whereof one acre and half an acre are at Uphosen, with the land of the Archbishop of Canterbury to the north, and another acre is at Wallesend between the land of the chapel of Overland east and land of Simon Gauson west.' This was to be sold to pay his debts, and he also gave his 'messuage at

Westmarsh called Peyndes with five roods of hempland adjoining and two acres of
pasture in one close of six acres of land opposite the messuage on the north side' to his
wife Joan for life and after her death to his sons William Roger and Thomas.

William Smith, husbandman of Ware, who died in 1485, ordered 'three roods of
land in the hamlet of Cokking to be sold to pay my debts', gave 'my tenement at Ware
called Philpotts, with one acre of land and one rood of hempland near the gate on the
south side, half an acre of pasture opposite the aforesaid gate, three acres called Hockedayes,
one acre and a half in the hamlet of Ware' to his wife Cecilie for life and then to his
son John, and gave to John 'my other messuage at Ware with four acres of pasture and
eight acres at Cokking'. In 1485, although William Peny's will gave each of his brother
Edmund's children 33s. 4d., he expressly stated that it was 'to be paid in corn and cattle'.

The will of Margery Uffington, who died in 1553, gave 'to the poor men's box
6s. 8d. and to five of the poorest folk in the parish 3s. 4d.'; it also contained a much
less usual bequest, a suit of body-armour, 'a man's harness, a breast plate, a back plate
and salett', to her son John Halet.

Not all the lands owned by one man always lay closely together, particularly if he
had painstakingly bought them little by little over the years. In 1550, Roger Omer of
Ware gave by his will to his wife Pleasance 'my pied red cow and all such household
stuff as she brought at our marriage, and Richard and Francis my sons shall pay her
yearly 6s. 8d.' He described 'the lands and tenements in Ash which I had with my first
wife, the mother of my four sons, and also have acquired', giving his son Richard

the messuage, garden, and lands bought from Forstall in which he now dwells, three acres of
land bought from Mr Boys, half an acre bought from Croker's widow, six acres bought from
William Gibbs, seven acres and three roods bought from Paul Richemond in the hamlet of Ware,
four acres bought from Mr Gason, one acre and a half bought from Baldocks, one acre and a
half situated in the brook near the way to Nell place, 10 acres at Grenedrove, two acres at
Wallesend, one rood of land situated between the Chantry and the heirs of Roger Seynt-
nicholas.

To his son William he gave

a messuage with garden at P'amor Street, 15 acres with another little messuage bought from
Cantisshe, 11 acres and three roods at P'amor Street bought from Mr Gason, 18 acres at Tripps
bought from Mr Boys, three acres and a half at Newclose, one acre and a half at Warehawthorn.

To his son Lawrence he gave

my messuage and garden at Nell with eight acres of land, 18 acres in Downefield bought from
Gibbs, two acres and three roods at Nasshe, my place at Hode with the garden, eight acres
bought from Mr Monings at Harman Street,

and to his son Francis

my messuage at Ware that I now dwell in with the garden and buildings of the same, three
acres next the messuage, six acres bought from Gason, 12 acres at Ivisbridge, nine acres at
Weltys, five acres at Corking, two acres in a close at Overland, two acres of brook land, three
acres in Warefield.

Occasionally a will reveals how bleak life could be for a widow. In 1479 William Collard left his 'mother Margery 20s. and 12 ewes, Isabella my sister a cow, and Roger, son of Thomas Collard of Preston, one ewe'. Yet, although he left 'six ewes, a cow and two calves' to his wife Joan, he provided only that she should have 'one low room on the north side of my tenement, with free coming and going' for life, and that after her death all should go to Thomas and John Collard. Sometimes a will was very precise: in 1556 William Pennye left to his wife Cecilie for life 'the house I dwell in with all the lands, except the new garden to son Simon', and went on to say that she should nevertheless have 'half the "Pome riall" growing in that garden, and half the next tree'.

John Saunders, canon of Wingham and vicar of Ash for more than 20 years, did not forget the parish when he died in 1509:

> To Ash Church a paxebred of silver and gilt, two cruets, a manual collectuary, two processioners which the wardens there be possessed of and have in their keeping, one coverlet lined with canvas, and towards buying a book called an Antiphonar for holydays and Sundays for the quire on the Vicar's side 40s.
>
> The Chapel of Richborough have one portuys printed, with a mass book that was Sir Thomas', the old priest's; and to the use of the same chapel 20s. to make them a new window in the body of the church.
>
> The Chapel of Overland have my little portes of fine parchment written by hand price 40s.; and to the use of the same chapel 40s. to make a better chalice or else a new window in the east end of the chapel.

The Church courts which dealt with the probate of wills required a 'true and perfect inventory' of the personal estate (that is, excluding houses and land) to be made immediately after the death. John Hunn, 'yeoman' of Ash, who died in May 1536, had little clothing and few personal effects: two stoles and a fur piece, together worth 8d.; two coats, a doublet and a jerkin, 20s.; and a purse, a girdle, a cap and three shirts, 3s.; £1 3s. 8d. in all. His house had only two rooms. In the bedchamber probably, were two 'transoms' and a feather bed, 6s. 8d.; a flock bed, 2s.; two coverlets, 6s.; four pillows, 16d.; nine pairs of sheets, 20s.; two tablecloths, four towels, and two 'pyllowcots', 4s.; four napkins, 8d.; five cushions and 'a banker', 4s. 8d.; and three chests, 3s. In his hall or kitchen were three pewter pots and a little bucket, three salt-cellars, 2s. 6d.; four brass pots and a chafer, 13s. 4d.; a brass pan, 2s.; a kettle 'in a furnesse', 4s.; two basins, two 'lavers', five candlesticks and two chafing-dishes, 7s. 4d.; a quern, 2s.; four tubs and a kneading-trough, 20d.; three trays and a bushel, 20d.; four stands, 16d.; 10 ale pots, 5d.; and a cupboard, 12s. In the fireplace, there were a pair of tongs, a rake, an andiron, two spits, a trivet, a 'cobyryn', two bills and two iron wedges, together worth 4s. 4d. He also possessed five silver spoons, worth 10s. Outside, there was firewood worth 3s. 4d.; growing crops—2 acres of wheat, 14s.; three acres of barley, 15s.; and three acres of 'podware', 10s.—a horse, worth 4s.; two cows and two heifers, 6s. Including two 'bene' (perhaps carts?) valued at 24s., John Hunn's total worth (apart from land, if he owned any) was £10 14s. 9d.

Seven

REFORMATION TO COMMONWEALTH

Soon after John Saunders' death the canons of Wingham neglected to provide a vicar at Ash. In 1535, Raymond Harflete of Ash wrote to Cardinal Wolsey's secretary:

> For the last 22 years ... the canons have usurped the vicarage to their own use, and let it to farm to temporal men who have put in such curates as ... were obtained by the farmer best cheap for his money. Within a quarter of a year we have had seven curates, which has caused much strife as we are 500 residents. By our complaint to the archbishop ... the canons were compelled to appoint us Sir Robert ... but the canons ... keep from him the tithes of wool and lamb ... and without them he cannot maintain hospitality. I desire you to have compassion on us.

It was this kind of complaint which stirred up the wrath of godly men against the Church, and which the king's servants saw might be turned to royal advantage. Rejection of the authority of Rome was followed by dissolution of monasteries and colleges, and the seizure of their wealth. When Wingham College was dissolved in 1546, among its possessions were listed

> the rent of one house in Ash called the Vicarage and three barns, one garden, one stable and other buildings; also one barn called Droves with 10 acres of land lying separately; also 1½ acres of glebeland lying next Crekyng; all the tithes from all the lands and tenements in Ash

valued at £76 3s. 4d., against which was set only the stipend of the 'chaplain serving the cure of the parish of Ash £7'. As part of the College's possessions, the chapels at Overland and Richborough were sold by the Crown in 1549. The properties of the two chantries in Ash church, the Chantry of Our Blessed Lady the Virgin and the chantry founded by John Septvans, had also been seized and sold in 1548. The chantry priests, William Hammond and Nicholas Rosse, evidently acted as curates so that it became necessary 'either to endow a vicar or else to appoynt some wellerned man to serve the cure there. And there is 430 houseling people [communicants] within the parish'.

The Ash properties of the Charity of Our Lady were scattered, many of them in very small pieces: a 'principal messuage or mansion' with three acres of land, 36 acres of marsh, seven pieces of land totalling 15 acres, six pieces totalling nine acres three roods, 36 acres more of marsh, six other pieces totalling 12 acres, and three more totalling two acres three roods (all let to Thomas Harflete), as well as one acre at Fisshepoole, a house in Ash Street and a virgate of land, eight acres of marsh, nine acres

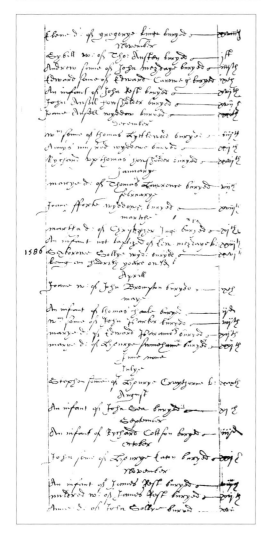

23   The Parish Register entry in 1586 for the burial of Sexborowe Solly. *Sexborowe Solly wyd: bury'ed xxxj [March] being on hundreth yeare ould.* She is the parish's first recorded centenarian.

in Longeland and at Harte, 17 acres of marsh, three acres and one rood of land, six acres and a half in Estfield, three acres and three roods of land, five roods, a 'small parcel of land', half an acre, two pieces totalling two acres and one rood, two acres, half an acre, five roods, two acres and three roods, and three and a half acres (all separately let to different tenants).

On Queen Mary's accession came a Catholic reaction. The rector of Adisham, John Bland, was a devout Protestant. Arrested in February 1554, imprisoned and condemned as a heretic, he was burned at the stake in Canterbury on 12 July 1555. Nothing so tragic happened at Ash; but the vicar, John Berymell, may have been one of those priests who had taken advantage of an Act of 1549 to marry, and now had to leave. In his place came William Lynch, himself a married man who had been deprived of the two Essex parishes of which he had been rector, and obliged to leave his wife Sarah behind in Essex. While here, in 1557, Lynch was ordered by the archdeacon 'to bord in some convenyent house and not in a comon alehouse'. At the same visitation the Ash churchwardens were ordered to repair the chancel, including the window glass, to build a new altar in the chancel of Our Lady and to furnish it, to provide a convenient place on which to set up the image of St Nicholas, and to provide a frontal fit for the high altar on holy days, a canopy for the consecrated elements, pins for the chrismatory for the holy oils, a grail, and a new christening, marriage and burial register, and to mend the font cover and provide a lock and key for it. Corresponding requirements imposed on other Kent parishes suggest that so far there had been very few deliberate changes inside the church at Ash since the 1530s.

In 1558, on the death of Queen Mary and the accession of Elizabeth I, Lynch was restored to his Essex benefices, and left Ash. But still it was not quite respectable for a priest to marry, even less for a woman to marry a priest. He and his wife both found life very difficult; in 1563 he was before his archdeacon's court for allowing her to 'daunse at the comon alehous'. Sarah admitted it, and also that she had 'herd herself accused of yvill fame'.

Worse was to come. In the following year he was ordered 'for myssinge 4 sermons to give to the poores box £1 6s. 8d.'; and 'for beyng a druncarde' to stand in 'the markett of Chellmesforde with a white shete and a white rodde in his hand confessing his fallts'.

For more than 30 years, England feared a Spanish invasion. Warning of danger was to be given by beacon fires lighted on hills, one on Beacon Hill in Woodnesborough. When at last the Armada was sighted in 1588, the train-bands of Kent, encamped at Northbourne, made a show of strength on the cliffs; while the reserves waited on Barham Downs. In 1602 Thomas Harflete of Molland was appointed 'Scoutmaster' for the St Augustine's Lathe of the county, with instructions for the 'watching' of its 17 beacons. East Kent was used to threats from the sea: 60 years earlier John Leland had written, 'Sandwich is neatly well walled where the town stondeth most in jeopardy of enemies. The residew of the town is diched and mudde waulled'.

Dissolution of the monasteries meant that the main source of help for the sick and poor had dried up. The state was forced, little by little, to try to fill the gap left by the Church. Successive Acts put the responsibility for dealing with poverty on the parishes. An Act of 1598 prohibited begging, and required every 'sturdy beggar' to be whipped 'until his body be bloody', and then sent back to his birthplace and there confined to a house of correction or gaol. The poor thought this oppressive. Henry Danyell of Ash (either this parish, or Ash near Sevenoaks) declared

> that he hoped to see such Warre in this Realm to afflict the riche men of this countrye to requite their hardnes of hart towards the poore; that the Spanyards were better than the people of this land and therefore he had rather that they were here than the rich men of this countrie; and that they had made such lawes for the sending of poore people into ther countryes where they were borne, that they that had made them would repent ...

Found guilty at Maidstone Assizes in July 1598 of uttering seditious words, he was ordered to be pilloried and remanded to gaol.

The parish officers took their new responsibilities seriously. About 1604 the Ash overseers paid William Deverson for attending to John Organ, a lame youth, and John Graye of Ash surgeon 'for attending the cure of Silvester Musred' and 'for curinge Hills daughters feet'. In July 1605, having already agreed with Graye that he 'should have yerely 20s. in respect of his pains taken and to be taken in surgerye with Silvester Musredd', they decided 'because of his povertye and wyfes being both blynd and himself so blynde as that he cannot now get sufficient thing towards his mayntenance' to pay him 40s. more 'yerely to be payd untyll such time as he shall be either otherwise provyded for whereby we shall fynde cause to decrease yt or by his further want to encrease yt'.

Fear of Catholic Spain led to anxiety for uniformity in religious practice. Battles of conscience between radical puritans and those who stood for more traditional forms of worship were reflected in events in Ash. In 1569 Widow Lode was suspected of witchcraft, and complaint was made that 'the minister ministereth the Communion in common bread and for default of a decent communion cup they minister it in a glass'. There were the usual human frailties: in 1573 the churchwardens complained that 'John Arrowsmyth, Matthewe Hughe, Robert Wyllington, John Oliver and John Upayce lyve from theire wieves, we know not where'.

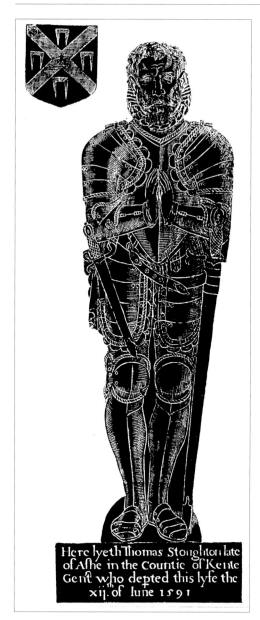

Here lyeth Thomas Stoughton late
of Afhe in the Countie of Kente
Gent who depted this lyfe the
xij. of Iune 1591

24 Thomas Stoughton of The Moat, Ash (d.1591).
His brass is not at Ash but in St Martin's Church,
Canterbury.

John Brooke, of Brooke Street, who
died—the last of his family—in 1582 and
who himself composed the inscription on
his memorial brass in Ash church, published
several translations from the French of
leading Protestant treatises.

In 1578 John Stybbinge was
appointed minister both of Ash and of
St Peter's, Sandwich. He was popular in
Sandwich: in 1581 the Corporation gave
him £10 'because he reads his lectures in
St Peter's for 8 months of the year whereas
other ministers only read for 4 months'.

In April 1583 Stybbinge and his wife
Brigitt appeared in the Canterbury
Consistory Court as witnesses in a suit for
defamation brought by Marjorie Harrison
against William Neame. Neame and his
wife had been living in May 1582 as
boarders in the Stybbinges' vicarage-house
at Ash. Brigitt Stybbinge said that, at the
dinner table, Neame had exclaimed, 'God's
wounds! Harrison's wife would have had
me lie with her, and I might have had my
carnal pleasure of her body if I would';
and that she was 'a common woman with
my brother Daniel Neame and to Master
Parker of Woodnesborough, for he was
the father of Harrison's eldest son'; and
that when her husband had rebuked him,
Neame had replied, 'What care I? For
when I came new down from London, I
went to Mr. Harrison when Mistress
Harrison did lie in, and I did bid him,
God send him joy of his wife's child'.
Stybbinge corroborated this, saying he was
persuaded in his conscience that the good
name and fame of Mistress Harrison were
impaired by Neame's slanderous speeches.
He added that some time before Christmas
1582, Neame had threatened him, and that he had complained to a justice, who had sent
his complaint to Quarter Sessions, where Neame had been bound over in the sum of
£100 to refrain from 'ill and slanderous speaking' against him or his wife.

Stybbinge was a puritan, and in 1585 the Corporation paid his expenses to visit
Archbishop Whitgift to ask permission to wear not a surplice but a black gown 'because

it is a general matter concerning the whole township, who would gladly be freed from the same, as they have been ever since her Majesty's reign'. He was one of the clergy who held out against subscribing to Whitgift's Articles of Religion, and in that same year his parishioners at Ash had to petition (evidently successfully) against his deprivation.

In 1602 Stybbinge was in the Consistory Court again, as an attesting witness to the will of Mistress Mercy Harflete which, he said,

> then being all written, she caused to be read, in her hall of the house of Mr. Thomas Harflete after supper, by Mr. Henry Harflete, her son, the sole executor, and after the same was so read did ratify publish and declare it to be her last will, and subscribed her mark and set her seal thereunto, being of perfect mind and memory and in good health.

He identified the will shown to him as the same will, the handwriting being all Mr. Henry Harflete's, with which he was well acquainted, and his own name being subscribed in his own hand. Evidently Mercy Harflete, despite her social position, could neither read nor sign her name.

In July 1608 Stybbinge wrote to George Newman, the Commissary General, following a plea from Robert Coulsonsacke's wife which

> this distressed woman hath made unto me touching her husband's crueltie towards her ... for gods sake to entreat you to pitie her miserie ... Beside his contynuale waywardnesse & many other injuries by strypes (as she reporteth) the last night he turned her out of doores, & wold not suffer her to come in againe. Neither is she now willing to go in howse to him any more, but in a desperate s[tan]ce rather to doe violence to herself being past all hope of worldly comfort ... wch to prvent I have afforded her this curtesye in writing to your worshipp in hope yt ye comfort of yr affabylytye towards her maye be a means to staye and prvent yt wofule & dangerous event I greatly fear.

Stybbinge married three times. His vicarage, on the south side of Ash Street, contained a 'halle', 'studdye', 'Kittchen', 'lytle buttry', 'drink house', 'mylke house', a parlour, six chambers (one used as a store), a 'well house', an apple house, a court with a lodge and wood-house, a wood-yard, a barn, a 'green close', and 'a frame for the vine'. When he died in 1615, he owned not only a collection of 'noted sermons with a small box bound with iron being about 100, 6s. 8d.', and a library of 308 books, 70 pamphlets, and sermons, valued (simply by their page size) together at £19 5s., three silver bowls, a silver beaker, six 'gilt Sylver' spoons and five silver spoons (£10 3s. 9d.), 'a mare, saddle & brydle' and a 'sydsaddle with 3 saddle clothes', but also, because he evidently farmed his glebe, '3 kine and 3 twelve monthynge calves', 'a sowe hogge', and 'a great coope with 20 Hens & Cocks', '12 bushells of wheate, 17 bushells of barly, & about 2 Bushells of Hempsede and about 10 quarters of Hemp', as well as '2 seams of barly at John Baxes' and 'A few beanes set'. He owned, besides, what may have been relics from the Spanish wars of his youth: 'a muskett, hedpece, sword, dagger with a bandaleere with a old caliver and daggr'.

Edward Chiselberry, curate of Stourmouth and also licensed in 1615 to teach in Ash, who died in March 1616 only a few weeks after Stybbinge, had lived in Ash much more simply; in a house with just a hall and one chamber, with two lofts above (one containing an old spinning wheel), and a milk-house. But he too had his own little

25 The brass to Christopher Septvans of Molland (d.1575) and his widow Mercy (d.1602).

library, 'A Book Case with 85 bookes in the same £2', and owned a cow with a 12-month-old calf, and four lambs. Stybbinge's 'wearing apparell both Lynnen and wollen' had been valued at £6 15s., with £5 in ready money, and his total personal estate had amounted to £129; Chiselberry's clothes were valued at only £1 13s. 4d, he had just 5s. 6d. in ready money, and his total estate was only £13.

Richard Howbacke, who died in March 1614, was described as a 'laborer'. Even so, his estate was worth £29. He lived in two rooms, but outside there was a milk-house, a drink house, a 'buntyng house' (where grain was separated from its chaff and stalks, and meal was sifted), a little court and moveable cow house, and he owned three cows, two heifers, two ewes, a ewe teg, and a sow. He too still kept his weapons by him: a spear, three swords and two daggers. Peter Hawkes, 'yeoman of Ash', died in May 1616. His farmhouse had a hall, parlour, kitchen, two butteries, and five chambers upstairs, with a wheat loft above, and a drink house, milk-house and cheese house. He possessed two linen wheels and a woollen wheel. He too kept a personal armoury: in the hall, besides his 'foulling peas' and 'burding pease', he had a musket, two swords, a 'houlbeard' and a 'hedpeas'. On the farm he had 28 acres of growing wheat, 32 acres of barley and 24 acres of pod-ware; four waggon-horses, three mares, a two-year-old and a yearling; nine cows with three two-year-old and five 12-month-old cattle; 27 ewes and 10 lambs, and 11 hogs, as well as some poultry.

At an inquest in May 1612 on Stephen Solley, an Ash blacksmith, the coroner's jury heard that on the night of 18 May John Meritt had been lying in bed at Ash when there was a noise outside. Looking out of the window, he had seen a white horse near the maypole which had been put up in the street near his house. Taking up a fowling-piece, he had fired at the horse, wounding it in several places, and also hitting Solley in the head. Solley had died next day, and the jury indicted Merrit on a charge of felonious killing, noting that the fowling-piece, a 'deodand', was worth 6s. 8d. At the Kent Assizes in July, Merritt was said to be still at large. In February 1613, at another inquest, the jury found that at Ash on 7 February, John Allen, a mason from Sandwich, had struck a 12-year old boy, Joseph Boykett, on the back with a stick and killed him, but at the Kent Assizes in March Allen was acquitted of felonious killing.

Sir Thomas Harflete ('otherwise Atchequer') of Molland died in September 1617. He had also rented the 'Great House' at St Martin's in Canterbury (now St Martin's Priory) at least since 1607, and evidently lived in some style. His purse, girdle and seal were valued at £20; his clothes—two suits of silk grosgrain, two of cloth, and one of stuff, a silk grosgrain cloak, two riding cloaks, five hats, a cape, six pairs of silk stockings and two other pairs, and a pair of velvet mittens—at £10, and his shirts, bands and other wearing linen at £5. In the house were a hall, parlour, study, kitchen, and buttery, five bed-chambers (and another in the garret) and a closet, and a gallery, as well as a gatehouse, a brew-house, a 'back house', and a stable with a loft above. His plate, both silver and silver-gilt, was valued at £55 15s. His own bedstead, with valance and tester, was curtained in crimson taffeta (£3), with a down bed, bolster, three pillows, feather bed and bolster, two blankets and a tapestry coverlet (£12). In his study he kept a 'horsman's armour' and four short pistols, and in the buttery 'A crosse bow & a Rack'. His coach and its harness, with the coach gelding and the two coach-horses, were valued at £35. In the stable, besides Sir Thomas's own mare and 'the gelding of Paramo', were another mare and a nag. Outside, he had six cows, 10 Welsh steers and two others, and 76 barren ewes and wethers, with 16 loads of hay and 60 'copp' of podware. He also had 120 'deal bords' and six thousand bricks, so building work was evidently in prospect.

Sir Thomas's surviving son Christopher Harflete succeeded to his estate, which also included Chequer and the manor of Chilton. Not too proud to engage in commerce, he saw it would be to his advantage to become a freeman of one of the Cinque Ports. In April 1620 he wrote from Molland to the mayor of Sandwich, asking him

> with the Jurats, common counsell and the rest of your assemblie, to make me free. I confess my affayres compell me to be free of some porte, but in my affection I am more inclined to yours. I assure you, my occasions cannot any way be prejudiciall to your towne, & my love & best offices, to my utmost power, shalbe willingly afforded.

Stybbinge's successor as curate at Ash, William Brigham, had been vicar of Wingham since 1607. His wife Margaret and Thomas Harflete's wife Elizabeth were sisters, daughters of Edward Oxenden of Brook in Wingham. Brigham had property at Walmestone, where he lived.

Moses Fletcher, formerly Stybbinge's parish clerk in Sandwich, was one of those who sailed in the *Mayflower* with the Pilgrim Fathers in 1620. Probably also puritans were Thomas Chambers, who farmed 112 acres at Overland, and his wife Richardene. They went out to the Plymouth Colony about 1637, with Thomas, Richard, Elizabeth, William and John Curtis, aged between 19 and six, her children by her first husband Thomas Curtis, yeoman of Ash, who had died in 1631. They settled first at Scituate, north of Plymouth, and then in 1642 moved further north to Gorgeana (renamed York in 1652), where in 1690 William Curtis was killed in a Indian massacre.

But as always there were some who cared less for spiritual matters. In the first years of Brigham's curacy, his churchwardens' fervour for their parishioners' proper keeping of Sunday as a day apart noticeably increased. Brigham was himself a puritan, and he no doubt encouraged them. In 1616, 1617 and 1618 they had reported several 'for profaning the Sabbath': James Bax, 'who spendeth the Sabaoth daie in gameing by which meanes he is very negligent in repairing to our church to divine service especially at Evening praier', Robert Hitchen from Goodnestone who had an orchard in Ash, 'by selling and pulling of cherries'; John Andrews by making hay, 'being told of it, he said ... it was but four groats matter'; Timothy Hart by 'his disorderly selling of beer and for suffering of people to be drinking and playing of cards and dice from the end of evening prayer to 10 or 12 o'clock at night'; and George Mode by 'disordering himself by overmuch drinking and then offending his neighbours by railing speeches, saying to the constables, "A pox on all Puritans!"'

In October 1620 they complained that 'Mr Crosyar, living in the house of Andrew Omer, hath preached in our parish church in the absence of our minister, without the knowledge of our minister or of us the churchwardens, and without shewing his licence to us.' On 22 November Crosyar was excommunicated. The churchwardens also presented Mercy Omer, 'the wife of Andrew Omer of Ash for not coming to church to give God thanks after her delivery of childbirth', and on 12 January 1621 she too was excommunicated.

Nathaniel Crosyar had graduated from Jesus College at Cambridge in 1613. He was, he said, a gentleman and, 'beside, a master of Arts, a minister and preacher of god's word'. He had lodged with Andrew and Mercy Omer in Ash since the summer of 1620, and had fallen in love with Mercy's 18-year-old younger sister Elizabeth Prior, living at Goldstone with her parents Daniel and Barbara Prior. They exchanged, he said

> abundant testimonies of love and affection, interchanging many amorous and sweet kisses and other love dalliances in a most fervent manner, embracing ardently one another as we lay together and, in the heat and fervour of our love, making many vehement and deep vows and solemn protestations of unfeigned love one to another and of marriage to be had and solemnised between us ... In token of her love and as a pledge of our intended marriage, [she] gave me a little gold ring, and with her own hand put it on my finger on condition that I should be her husband,

and

> several gifts or tokens were on both sides most thankfully received and accepted of ... I, taking Elizabeth by the hand and so holding her by the hand and speaking to her, used these words, or the like in effect and substance: Elizabeth, I take thee to my lawful wife and do promise thee marriage in time convenient, in the name of the Father the Son and Holy Ghost; and then loosing hands Elizabeth took me by the hand and looking at me used these or the like words: Nathaniel, I take thee to my lawful husband and do likewise promise to marry with thee in time convenient, in the name of the Father the Son and the Holy Ghost and then we lovingly kissed and embraced each other ... Neither did she strive out of maidenly modesty to conceal or hide her affection or the violence of her passion therein, but laid it open to the world in such manner that everyone almost thereabouts took notice thereof, and it was much talked of in the parish of Ash.
>
> Being told that Richard Solly had been or was suitor unto her for marriage, [she] inveighed bitterly against Solly and called him Gunbelly Ass with other foul terms and titles, and protested that she would never marry with him, for that she was contracted and sure to me, and said that she had told Richard Solly so much.

26 This mural monument to Sir Thomas Harflete of Molland (d.1617) and his second wife Bennet, was no doubt put up by Sir Thomas himself soon after Bennet's death in 1612, for he later married a third wife.

Elizabeth's parents had given their blessing on the intended marriage, but then her father died. Her widowed mother decided she should marry Solly, the 22-year-old son of John and Christian Solly of Pedding. On 14 May 1621 a licence for that marriage was obtained, and Solly and Elizabeth were married at Woodnesborough the same day. Crosyar was outraged. (He had cause to be: under English common law all that was required (then, and until 1753) to contract a valid marriage was that the couple should take each other as husband and wife in the presence of a cleric. It was not until 1861 that the Court decided that the cleric must be a third person, so that a wedding performed by a cleric between himself and a woman was void.) On 18 May Crosyar applied to the Consistory Court to have Elizabeth's marriage to Solly set aside, on the ground that she was already contracted in marriage to Crosyar himself, and perhaps also asked for an order for specific performance of his own contract of marriage with her by compelling its celebration in church. At the Court hearing on 13 June, he said, 'I and Elizabeth Prior were and are lawfully contracted in matrimony, and indeed man and wife together'. Tantalisingly, neither the result of his application, nor what happened to him thereafter, is known. Richard Solly, 'yeoman, of Ash', died in 1638, leaving personal estate of just £23.

In 1625 the Ash churchwardens turned on Brigham, for 'not reading service on holy days, and living on a farm of his own at Wingham', outside the parish. He replied that he had 'until of late read divine service on those days, and because he saw very few, and sometimes none, come to the church, he hath desisted', and that his house at Walmstone was 'nearer to the church than some part of his parishioners'. Next year they reported that an unlawful conventicle—a debate on doctrine—had taken place at John Bax's house at Ash, attended by two separatist ministers, John Fenner and Matthew Gilver, by George Huntley the puritan rector of Stourmouth and his curate Fellowes, and by a crowd of local people.

In 1618 James I had acknowledged the 'general complaint of our people that they were barred from all lawful recreation and exercise upon the Sunday's afternoon after the ending of all Divine Service' and published his Declaration of Sports, ordering that once they had attended service 'our good people be not disturbed, letted or discouraged from any lawful recreation'. In 1638 Charles I ordered this Declaration to be read from all pulpits, and it seems that Brigham was one of those who refused. The churchwardens' accounts for 1634 included receipt of 'A peny of every on of thouse that Reseave the Comunion towards the providing of Breed an wine for the same which ceam to 2li.6s. 4d in that yeare', and 'payd for bread an wine for the Estar Communions beeing 6 in numbar And the partyes 623 which Reseved for Estar in the yeare 1634'. The parish clerk, Simon Barrow, was paid 4s. 'for tacking the Communicats names all the yeare munthly'. It must have been Barrow who in 1635 listed the names of 36 men 'which occupie no land in the parish of Ash bute only dwell in Cotages'.

The churchwardens paid £7 'to Parkeson the paynter for the sentenses and the King's arms and the doing of the Pilars and font' in 1637. But Archbishop Laud was not satisfied. In December 1637 they were ordered to

> take away the seat at or under the east wall and window of their quire or chancel, and provide a new and decent Communion table, with a better or more seemly carpet or cloth to it, and place it at the east end of the quire, fencing it off with a decent and seemly rail to stand before it nearest the quire for the parishioners to come up into at the time of the celebration of the Sacrament, and thus, being accommodated with some convenient thing to kneel upon, to receive the same, the minister during the time of the celebration keeping within the rail.

Brigham was deprived by the Archbishop, and replaced by William Lovelace (cousin to Richard Lovelace, the Cavalier poet who wrote 'Stone walls do not a prison make, Nor iron bars a cage'). One difficulty was that the 'the Vicaridge house in Ashe is very smale and rotten'. In March 1641, just after Laud had been impeached by the Commons and committed to the Tower, the parishioners petitioned Sir Edward Dering, a Kent member of Parliament and chairman of its Committee for Religion, about the Archbishop's treatment of Brigham:

Ere long, his Grace will be past grace: His unworthy dealing with our parish has wrought the decay of religion among us ... We humbly desire that Mr. Brigham may be re-established in Ash, he being illegally displaced ... and the Vicarage-house new built, and the pigeon house there repaired for him, and made fit for a reverent minister to reside in and to live with comfort amongst us.

In September 1641 the House of Commons declared that communion tables should be removed from the east end of churches, and the rails destroyed, that bowing during service should cease, and that there should be no dancing or other recreation on the Lord's day.

In May 1641 the Commons, 'finding to the great grief of their hearts that by the designs of priests and Jesuits there are plots and conspiracies to subvert the fundamental laws of the Kingdom and to introduce Arbitrarie and Tryannicall government by the most Pernicious Councels', had proposed that everybody should be *required* to subscribe to a protestation to maintain the true reformed Protestant religion. But, because the Lords would not agree, the Commons could only ensure that all men over 18 in every parish in England were *invited* to do so. On 20 February 1642 Lovelace made a return to Parliament of 'The names of them in the parish of Ash in East Kent that have taken the Protestation'; there were 279 names, with his certificate that 'All they whose names are contained in this paper have taken the protestation, according to order from the Parliament; And they did it willingly and cheerfully. And none in our parish of Ash did refuse it. Nor do I know any that have escaped my diligence.'

Although in time Brigham was restored to Ash, it seems that nothing was done to repair the vicarage-house. In July 1647, four Parliamentary commissioners met 'at the sign of the Red Lion in Ash Street'; they found

upon the said Parsonage one Tenement, timber built being much out of repair, containing below stairs four rooms and above stairs four rooms, part tiled and part thatched; with two barns thereunto belonging, thatched and timber built and walled about with boards, the one containing seven bays and the other four bays; one stable, thatched; and one dove-house, tiled, out of repair, and unreplenished; one apple orchard containing in it about 40 trees, viz., pear-trees, apple-trees and plum-trees; the land in the orchard and places and that whereon the house and barns stand is paled against the King's highway and the other fences are dyked and teened, the whole containeth three acres more or less, worth £6, being glebe; the aforesaid premises abutteth upon the land of Thomas Harflett Esq' west and north, and upon the King's highway south and east; standing upon the premises 11 small trees which we value at 10s

During the Civil War, Ash parishioners' loyalties were divided. Thomas Peke of Hills Court was a Royalist, and one of those who went to Sandwich in 1648 to try to enlist support for the King's cause, but in 1652 Oliver Cromwell himself was in the town, and Thomas St Nicholas, of The Mote at Hoaden, was very much on the side of Parliament. He was 'agent in this part of Kent for Parliament for raising troops to fight against the King'. Lawyer to Sir Michael Livesey, one of the regicides, he was a member of both the Commonwealth Parliaments, a justice of the peace, a fierce Presbyterian, and an influential local figure. When in July 1657 Daniel Ralph asked for a victualler's licence at the *Chequer Inn* for billeting soldiers and lodging strangers, Quarter Sessions referred the application to St Nicholas.

Use of the Prayer Book had been forbidden by a Parliamentary Ordinance of 1645. In its place had been prescribed 'A Directory for the Public Worship of God', and the Ash churchwardens duly 'paid too Shillings for ye Directory Book'. The Directory required 'baptism to be dispensed in the face of the congregation where the people may most conveniently see and hear, and not in the place where fonts in the time of Popery were unfitly and superstitiously placed'; no doubt why the churchwardens accepted £1 'from Mr St Nicklas for ye funt stone' in 1656. In the same year they paid 8d. 'for on oure glas' and 1s. 'ffor a fframe for ye houre glass', perhaps signs that sermons were growing longer. In 1652 they had also 'pd to Thomas Browne for 3 years keeping the doggs out of Church £1 4s.'

Under the Commonwealth, human nature changed very little. In 1652 the church-wardens 'pd for Carring of the Timber for the Stockes house and rayles 10s.', and received 'ffor a ffine ffor Mr. William Baker his profane swearing in ye pish of Ash 6s. 8d.' and from Richard Sanders 'for pfane swearing two oaths or upon ye second commiccion 6s. 8d.'—he had paid 16s. 8d. 'for 5 oaths' the previous year. They had £1 'of Edward Philpot for his forfeiture for selling of beere without license', and 'of Thomas Bax junior & Simon Brice either of them 3s. 4d. appece for there penaltie for remayning Tipling in ye house of ye said Edward Philpott Contrary to ye statute in yt case made', so it was not surprising that they also collected 'of Edward Philpott for 3 oaths 10s.' In 1653 Richard Boxe of Ash admitted at Quarter Sessions that he had stolen a sheep from Thomas Beere, and sold it to a butcher.

From May 1641 no further entries of baptisms, marriages or burials were made in the parish register, until Simon Barrow the parish clerk was elected 'Register' for Ash (and seven neighbouring parishes) in November 1653, and started a new register of births, marriages and deaths. Barrow also practised as a surveyor, and at least three of his estate maps have survived.

Brigham died in 1653, and in October 1657 the Parliamentary Trustees for Min-isters presented William Nokes to the curacy of Ash. He was still only 21, but a graduate of St John's, Cambridge, and 'esteemed as a man of good abilities'. The churchwardens did what they could for clergy dispossessed by Parliament, giving 2s. 6d. 'In releife to Anoulld minestar' and 1s. 'to a pore minester'.

There were recurrent local outbreaks of plague. In the 'great sickness' of 1644, more than a thousand people died in Sandwich; and the county justices suggested ways to prevent the townspeople going to church at Ash or Woodnesborough for fear of 'a hazard of infecting the country which hath been very liberall toward the poor infected'. Thomas Peke's younger brother Matthew died in 1659 when Mayor of Sandwich, in another epidemic which killed 170 townspeople as well as 100 soldiers recently landed from Dunkirk.

EIGHT

THE RESTORATION

On the Restoration of Charles II in 1660, the Ash churchwardens 'paid to the Ringers on Crownation day' and to Goodwife Leggatt, John Durrant and Daniel Ralph 'for the Ringers the same day' no less than £1 18s. 2d. Besides £3 1s. 'for setting up of the king's armes', they paid William Cooke 'for mending the Communion table and setting up two benches 3s. 4d.' and 'for glue for the communion table 4d'. In 1664 they bought back the ancient font. Then, and for many years to come, every royal occasion involved ringing the church bells, and the churchwardens were expected to quench the ringers' loyal thirst: in 1665 they paid 'To the Ringers when the duke of yorks men laye in Ashe 6s.', and in 1672 there was 'given the Ringers when the queene was att Sandwitch 10s.'

Nokes, who had not been episcopally ordained, was ejected from his curacy. Afterwards, 'he contunu'd Preaching here and there as Opportunity offer'd: but dy'd in a few Years'. He was replaced at Ash by Robert Wilkinson, who stayed less than a year. Wilkinson's successor, James Benchkin, had himself been dispossessed by Parliament in 1643 of his parish at Kelsall in Suffolk. Benchkin had a family home at Poulton, just outside the parish, where he lived, as Brigham had done at Walmestone. Barrow's register entries continued methodically until March 1661, when Benchkin took over from him. On 14 April Benchkin entered Barrow's burial, 'An old man and the parish Clarke'. He also entered in the old register the baptisms between 1641 and 1661 of Peter Peke's eight children.

The nonconformist tradition persisted in Ash. Charles Nicholls, an Independent minister from Adisham, officiated at services held in houses belonging to Thomas St Nicholas, Stephen Bing and John Mockett. St Nicholas was a thorn in the flesh of Benchkin, who complained in 1664 that he was

> a wilful disturber and interrupter of divine service in that part of the Common Prayer Book which concerns the burial of the dead ... Accompanying the corpse of one Widdow Solley to the church, the corpse was no sooner set down but he laid his hand upon it, and desired some of the standers by to put it presently into the grave. I ... again and again did desire him to forbear ... He nevertheless continued with his hat on his head, urging some of the standers by to pull the corpse presently into the grave. Which being done he presently hasted away, not staying to have the service read.

St Nicholas was trying to impose, despite the new Book of Common Prayer, the practice laid down by the Directory: 'When any person departeth this life let the dead body, upon

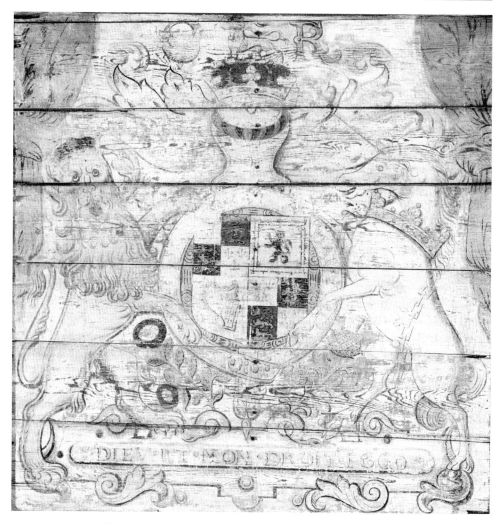

27   Royal Arms of Charles II, 1660, in St Nicholas Church.

the day of burial, be decently attended from the house to the place appointed for public burial, and there immediately interred, without any ceremony.' Benchkin bemoaned St Nicholas' 'manifest contempt of authority, the scandal of some, and the evil example of others upon many of whom, by his eminence as a lawyer and a person of fair estate, he hath no small influence'.

In 1672, when dissenting congregations were at last able to apply to license their meetings, 50 licences were issued in Kent in the first year. Two were for Ash, for meetings of Presbyterians and Independents.

Archbishop Sheldon was an old man. When he decided in 1677 to require a return from every English parish to show, as he believed, that widespread fears of growth of both Protestant dissent and Roman Catholicism were exaggerated, he asked Henry Compton, the Bishop of London, to organise what became known as the 'Compton Census'. In due course Benchkin reported from Ash that there were 'by common account rich and poore about two hundred and twenty families inhabiting therein' (an over-estimate, to judge from the Hearth Tax return of 13 years earlier), that he believed there was 'no one popish recusant knowen, or suspected to be such', but that there were 'about twenty families of knowen and professed sectaries of all sects inhabiting therein, and at least an hunderd of particular persons'; and that, although there had been 'heretofore by common report some hunderds of communicants', there were not then above 60 or 70 at most. He added sadly, 'Some out of obstinacy, and others out of carelesse and atheisticall presumptions wilfully absenting themselves from the publike service and communion of the church, do in times of liberty turne deafe ears to all exhortations and instructions to the contrary'.

Benchkin died in 1679, and three years later, in 1682, his successor as curate, Alexander Mills, reported to Archbishop Sancroft's chaplain that Valentine Dilnot, a Brownist, had become reconciled to the Church, and he hoped Francis Holt, an Anabaptist, might do so. He added, 'I have several others of the same sort in my parish'.

In 1680 Mills had also been appointed minister of St Clement's, Sandwich. In consequence he had to do battle with the churchwardens of Ash. In 1683 they presented him for 'not supplying the cure of Ash above once a Sunday'. He replied that he 'did for about three years together have morning service, and not above five or six persons to hear prayers, and upon their request have served it only with afternoons, unless it be on a sacrament day, and then he serves forenoon only'. He was ordered to read both morning and evening prayer, either personally 'or by some other person sufficiently allowed thereto'. Three years later the churchwardens presented him 'for not residing in the parish, nor administering the Sacrament or supplying the cure on 15th July 1686', but he replied that Mr. Piggott, minister at St Mary's and St Peter's in Sandwich, and Mr. Burville, minister at Whitfield and Tilmanstone, had done so. In 1689 the churchwardens tried again, this time making five complaints: that Mills did not reside in the parish; that he had failed to church Elizabeth Stonard, Alice Horne and Elizabeth Saffery after the births of their children; that he had not said the burial service over Robert Martin's daughter Elizabeth; and had not baptised Thomas Lacy's child or (about six years previously, in 1683, and although the boy was dangerously ill) Thomas Hatcher, son of Henry Hatcher, a church-warden. Evidence was given in support of the allegations by Hatcher himself, and by four parishioners; John Jull, the Ash sexton, Maria Bax and Sara Brett, both aged 20, and Alice Horne. Twenty-year old John Luckocke of Woodnesborough said

> Some time since last Christmas, Thomas Lacy had a child to be baptised. On a Sunday the child was brought to the church and, there being no minister to read prayers neither in the forenoon nor afternoon, the child was carried home unbaptised. Some few days afterwards Henry Gardner's wife died in Ash and was there buried. There being a minister to bury the corpse, Lacy's child was brought down to the church, and there was baptised by the minister. I know this to be true for I stood as a godfather to the child.

In reply, Mills said he had resided as much as he could, 'there being no house for him in the said parish', by reading divine service and preaching on Sundays and adminis-tering the sacrament at the appointed times, and had been ready to visit the sick, baptise children and bury the dead upon notice from parishioners. He lived in Sandwich 'about two miles distant', and for most of the time he had been curate of Ash, 'his Curate of

St Clement's had been resident in Ash and performed all ministerial offices'. He claimed the proceedings against him were malicious, that John Saffery had 'from time to time and in divers manners traduced and defamed' him, and had once done so 'in so gross a manner that to avoid the prosecution of the Law, he acknowledged his fault' in his own hand before four witnesses. Mills in turn asked the Court to consider his own complaint that Saffery had not presented

> several notorious crimes in the said parish committed, contrary to his oath and certain knowledge, by which he incurs the manifest guilt of perjury. Particularly he has not presented the most scandalous neglect of the not receiving the Sacrament at Easter, which was not received by most of the parishioners, to the offence of God and all good men.

As early as 1660 Richard Wallis of Ash had been arrested for his Quaker beliefs. Even after the Toleration Act of 1689, although Quakers were no longer required to attend church, their refusal to pay tithes led to distraint being levied on their possessions. John Love and Martha Bax were married in Ash church on Christmas Day 1664. In due time, their eldest son John was apprenticed to a shoemaker in Canterbury, and there became a Quaker. Because of his beliefs he refused an oath of allegiance to the king and, with a fellow apprentice, was committed to prison. Upon his release, still aged only 18, his parents, as he reported, 'made suit for the residue of my time of apprenticeship, and took me (with consent of my master) home to them, and set me up of my trade by them'. His parents expected him to accompany them to church at Ash. His father 'laboured to have me with him to hear the priest', and was angry; 'Sometimes I have expected him to have beaten me'. On 26 June 1684 he was presented by the church-wardens 'ffor not frequenting his parish church to heare divine service and for not receiving ye Sacrament'. As a result, he was excommunicated, 'which was no small terror to my father'. For all that, he gradually persuaded his whole family to become Quakers.

His father's house at Guilton had a barn and four acres of land and now, as a Quaker, he refused to pay his church cess or his tithe. He described what then happened in a pamphlet entitled

> The Suffering Case of John Love, of Ash, near Sandwich in Kent; who for his Conscientious refusal to Pay Twenty Shillings for one years tythe was prosecuted to a sequestration by Francis Wood, who alledged he was excited thereto by Daniel Small, Steward to the Widow Cartwright.

Wood, a substantial farmer from Richborough, was one of the churchwardens who obtained a sequestration order from the Court. They 'pd for sining ye order & Warant to destrain ye quakers for ye Church cess 2s.' On 15 January 1696, in midwinter, their attorney, John Plumer, sent in the bailiffs 'to levy and carry away all the goods in the house worth taking away and all his corn, except about one Gallon of barley'. Wood later regretted his own part in it. 'Tis said Francis Wood is very sorry his name was ever concerned in this matter; saying, that if he thought they would have been so severe, he would rather have suffered great loss than to have had his name used therein.'

It was difficult to get men to carry out the order. John Horne, the master of the poorhouse, 'being desired to be appraiser, refused, and would not be concerned in it for five pounds'. Gamaliel Tomlen, a joiner, also refused, and said he 'would not meddle if they would give him Forty Shillings'. Richard Friend, a carpenter, was asked to take down the beds but refused, and told John Love that he would help the Quakers, but not the sequestrators, with anything that needed taking down. John Grigg was asked to help 'and he should be paid for half a days work', but he too refused, and went away 'concerned to behold their ungodly deeds'.

But others were less reluctant. Daniel Small, steward to the new Guilton tithe owner Mrs. Cartwright, who himself became a churchwarden later in the year, was in charge. Perhaps Mrs. Cartwright was not then living in the village and knew nothing of what was being done by Small in her name, for Love wrote that 'he shiftily said it was his ladies act and not his; but he was told that his lady as he called her would be made acquainted with it to know if she would own such an unchristian act'.

Plumer, the attorney, and John Petly of Guilton, the former tithe owner, were both present. So was George Waker, described by Love as 'a wicked, envious man against Friends as by his behaviour did appear, by his searching out things beyond any of the rest'. Love warned them 'to take heed what they did, for some of them had grey hairs'. Small, he said, was 'very turbulent in his behaviour'; his servants tore and broke down Love's goods, threw them out of the window 'as if it had been where a house is on fire', and

> took my victuals and threw it down, some in a chair, and some on the ground, and stepped over it, which came so over them, that two of the bailiffs wept to behold such oppression; and one of the bailiffs seeing a dog going to it, drove him away; and one of them cried out at Small's cruelty, so that he was troubled to get his work accomplished.

After this 'havock and stir', Love took his food and 'set it forth on an old stool what was made to set bees on, but was then my best table, and desired the sequestrators to eat and drink of such as they had left me, after their hard toyl and labour to ruin me.' His daughter Martha wrote

> They came with three bailiffs and took and carried away to the value of £57 and upwards in goods, so that my father hath not a bed to lie on, nor a blanket to cover himself, nor scarce a chair to sit in, nor scarce necessary thing, nor no corn left by them, except about a gallon of barley.

She recounted how that night the family lay

> all six of us, in good clean straw beds, as was left us in the barn: and blessed be the Lord, we felt his living presence to make our straw-beds as easie to us as if it had been a bed of down; and in this we could all rejoice, and did rejoice, finding better goods left than was taken away.

She was much encouraged that two of the bailiffs had been so horrified by what they were doing, and so impressed with her family's patience, that they had resolved never again to meddle in such a case. In 1697 John Marbrook's will expressed the hope that after paying various legacies there would be money enough left over to build a Quaker Meeting House in Ash or Preston. John Love's eldest son John returned to Canterbury. In 1700 he registered a new Meeting House at Swalecliffe. He was still suffering for his beliefs, and by 1703 was writing an account of his experience in the stocks. But in Ash, in January 1707, Henry Minter was baptised at the age of 32, evidently another Anabaptist returned to the Anglican fold.

The churchwardens continued to act as the guardians of their parishioners' morals. In 1699, 'John Baseborn son of Jno Kendal and Eliz: Gray' was baptised, and the churchwardens 'pd Tho: Eastland for ye use of his sheet, And returning ye Order to Court when Eliz: Gray did penance 1s.'. Nor were they themselves immune from being presented. In 1706 unspecified allegations were made against John Webb 'some of which are of a very heinous and scandalous nature and contain such matter that he ought to be deprived of his office of churchwarden'. Asked whether he could 'purge himself' of the complaint or whether he would resign, Webb answered that 'some persons would swear anything & yt he was not guilty of ye said matter, but was willing to renounce the said office of churchwardenship & did renounce the same'. Pretty certainly the complaint was about his relationship with Damaris Maple who was living in his house and had at least one bastard child, but who was herself a woman of property and when she died in November 1707 appointed 'my master John Webb senr and his son John Webb junr' as executors of her will, desiring them 'to take this special care and trust upon them as to see my son [Richard Oyne] well and orderly brought up'.

Lady Wilde, widow of a Recorder of London, and her son William lived at Goldstone. Her private chaplain, Charles Maddison—like about 400 other clergy, eight bishops, and Archbishop Sancroft himself—had in 1689 felt unable to take a fresh oath of allegiance to William and Mary, because he felt himself irrevocably bound by his oath to the abdicated James II, and had consequently been deprived of his vicarage of St Andrew, Newcastle-on-Tyne. Many 'non-jurors' were reduced to great poverty, and a number, like Maddison, found places as domestic chaplains.

From the time of Queen Anne there have survived a census of the 1,191 Ash parishioners in 1705 (made for a tax on births, marriages, burials and bachelors), and a diary kept by Thomas Minter of Weddington.

Through the night of 26-7 November 1703 there raged 'the terrible tempest which we call by way of distinction the Great Storm'. As its fury passed across the country 'trees went down in battalions, the lead roofs on cathedrals and parish churches were rolled up like carpets; in many places scarce a chimney remained standing, not a roof uninjured. Boats were flung out of river beds, carriages thrown over hedges into the fields.' But the most terrible events occurred off the coast of Kent, in the crowded anchorage in the Downs off Deal and Sandwich Bay. Here, the Royal Navy lost 15 warships as well as smaller craft and 1,500 seamen, and several hundred merchant ships must have gone down. Only the skill and courage of the ships' crews averted worse losses. Indeed, their seamanship saved England, for it was wartime, and in France it was at first supposed that England had lost her entire fighting fleet. At Weddington, Thomas Minter wrote up his diary,

> Ye 27th of November in ye Morning was a terrible storm of wind which by relations drove 100 saile of ships out of the Downs and Dammiged (little or much) ye greatest part of houses and barns in East Kent (if not in England) viz. Ye River of Thames it staved 200 saile of ships 1,000 trawlers and wherries and sunk and dammiged 700,000 quarters of corn; in ye Cyty it killed a great many people and broke down or at least dammiged almost all ye houses in ye City.

On 3 November 1705 he noted, 'ye widdow Prince was hanged without Canterbury gate at Sandwich', probably the woman whom William Boys said was 'hanged for the murder of her bastard child'. At Ash the stocks were still in use, for in 1674 the churchwardens 'paid John Markes for mending the stocks house and Boards about the same 2s.', and again in 1738 'p^d John Eastland for Mending the Stocks house'. But if life was often harsh, there were gentler times, too: Minter also recorded 'June ye 23 1708 Wee beat Ash Street at Crickets'.

In 1709 the churchwardens 'pd Thos: Minter for writing ye Register into the parchment book for one and thirty years back to this time £1 10s.', and on 'April ye 27th 1710 At a Vestery Held at ye Lion it was ordered … that ye Ringers have no More than half a Crown for Ringing on ye Common Ringing Days Allowed by ye Church-wardens … that Everyone that Comes to a Parish Meeting shall spend his own money.' In 1711 John Shocklidge, who had been curate of Ash since 1691, suddenly refused to pay the church rate assessed on him. The churchwardens, put in an embarrassing position, were ordered by the Vestry to take the opinion of Counsel. Perhaps the poor man had become mentally deranged. He was buried at Ash on 30 January 1713, and it has been said that he drowned in the river Stour.

Ash shared in the great rebuilding of timber-framed houses in brick which took place all over south-east England after 1660. Molland, Chequer, The Moat south of the church, Weddington and Uphousden were all faced in brick, often with the 'Flemish' gables which were a feature of new houses at Goldstone, Guilton and Westmarsh. Of the larger houses in the parish perhaps only three, Brooke House, Paramour and Wingham Barton, retained their exposed timbers. This was very different from Sandwich, described in 1697 as 'a sad old town all timber building … run so to decay that except one or two good houses its just like to drop down the whole town'.

On the death of Thomas Harfleet in 1672, his daughter Aphra succeeded to the Ash estates of his uncle Sir Christopher Harfleet, who had died in 1662. She conveyed them to her husband John St Ledger, and they were put up for sale. They were described in

A perticular of Divers messuages and Lands to be sold in Ash-next-Sandwich in Kent …

A ffaire messuage called Molland wth a small court or yard before ye house all but a litle fenced in wth a Brick wall a litle brick house over the gate of the yard very handsome a garden fenced in wth a Brick wall two orchards two barnes a stable & an outhouse of bricke 230 acres of land arrable pasture & Marsh wth a small wood rent payable at Mich & Lady Day Rich: Wells tenn^t at per ann. £161 10s.

A ffaire messuage called Chequer one half Brick other tymber wth other necessary houses & moted round and other necessary houses about it wth 100 acres of land arrable & pasture & Marshe payable at Michmas & Lady Day und^r rented at per ann. £100.

A ffaire messuage at Gilton Towne in Ash 2 barnes 1 stable 1 maulthouse 130 acres of land arrable pasture & marsh & 1 small messuage wth outhouses 2 acres of land, one other small house wth a small shot of ground to itt rent £125 per ann payable Mich: & Lady day John Petley tennant.

A small messuage or tenem^t at Gilton Towne in Ash wth outhouses thereunto belonging 28 acres of land arable & pasture & one other small house & ½ an acre of land to it, payable ½ yearely at Lady day and Mich: Wm Price tennant £32.

A small tenem^t or dwellinghouse in Ash streete wth an orchard & land to it whereby the Court is usually held rent and quitt rents of the Manner Called Chilton and Chequer at per Ann £6.

Two other Small Tenem^{ts} in Ash Streete wth the ground to them est. at £4.

That the houses of the ffower ffarmes are all substantiall and in good repaire and that the lands of all those ffarmes lye all together & none betwixt them but Highwayes. The lands are all inclosures well fenced each ffarme in it selfe, except the Marsh Lands. That the lands are very good and sowne every yeare. Timber upon the premises worth £200.'

John and Aphra St Ledger sold the last of the Harflete estates at Ash in the 1690s. In 1695 Dr George Thorpe, rector of Bishopsbourne and Ickham, and once Sancroft's chaplain, bought Chequer. When he died in 1719 he left it to Emmanuel College, Cambridge, of which he had long been a Fellow and recently Master-elect, to endow scholarships for poorer undergraduates studying divinity, 'preference being given to sons to orthodox ministers of the Church of England and diocese of Canterbury, and such as are brought up in the King's School, Canterbury'.

Between 1662 and 1688 Hearth Tax was an important source of government revenue, 'it being easy to tell the number of hearths, which remove not as heads or polls'. Each hearth was taxed at the rate of 2s. a year. Those too poor to pay parish rates, or who occupied premises worth less than 20s. a year, or whose possessions were not worth more than £10, were exempt. The returns for Ash for 1662 and 1664 have survived, and the 1664 return lists those who were exempt. In 1662 tax was charged on 83 households, of which 32 had three or more hearths. Only one (Thomas St Nicholas' house at Hoaden) had seven; four had five; five had four; 19 had three; 21 had two; and 30 had only a single hearth.

In 1664 there were 106 households in the parish, and tax was charged on 81 of them. Of those, only 24 had three or more hearths; one (St Nicholas' again) had seven; two had six; six had five; seven had four; eight had three; 23 had two; and 34 had one only. Of the 25 households whose occupiers were exempt, two had three hearths, five had two, and 18 had only one.

In 1664 Stephen Cleaveland was taxed on six hearths (up from five in 1662) at Brooke Street, and John Bax for six (up from four) at Westmarsh. In both 1662 and 1664, Henry Harfleet at Hills Court, Stephen Bax at Molland, and Thomas Young at Goldstone were each taxed on five hearths. In 1664 three others were also taxed on five hearths: Joseph Wells at Chequer (up from four in 1662), John Proud, gent. at The Moat in Ash Street (Moat Farm), and Richard Solly, probably at Guilton parsonage (both up from three). In both 1662 and 1664 'Widdow' Foat at Cop Street, Thomas Brown at Hoaden, and Richard Morton were each taxed on four hearths. In 1664 four others were also taxed on four hearths: 'Widow' (Margaret) Solly at Pedding, John Petley at Guilton, and Robert Jefford, probably also at Guilton (all up from three in 1662), and Ralph Leggatt at Paramour Street (down from five in 1662). Six households were taxed on three hearths in both 1662 and 1664: Stephen Stringer at Goshall, William Taylor at Weddington, David Denn at Guston, and Mr. John Gibbon, John Bax and John Durrant, probably all in Ash Street. The other two households taxed on three hearths in 1664 were John Carr at Richborough (down from four in 1662), and David Saffry at Nash (also down from four in 1662, but he may have moved house).

The tax involved the churchwardens in some entertaining: in 1674 they 'pd in Expence upon the Harth Collector when wee got him to take An Acount of the names of the poore people which are exemted from paying 1s. 2d.' They were themselves assessed on the hearth in the church which warmed the schoolroom, and noted in 1687 'Pd yᵉ Chimney man for 4 halfe yeares arrears for the Chimney in the Church Loft 4s.'

In March 1662 Michael Wood, a cordwainer and Ash shopkeeper, died. His stock of ready-made shoes was worth 45s. His groceries included white sugar (worth 6d. a pound), brown sugar (3d.), currants (5¾d.), prunes (300 lb. of them at 1½d.), butter, cheese, oatmeal, bacon, suet (white and brown), red herrings, oils, vinegar, spices (cinnamon, cloves, ginger, indigo, mace, nutmeg and 'wormeseed'), saffron and tobacco. He also stocked hardware and ironmongery: earthenware pots, iron pans, bottles, glasses, knives, nails, beeswax, turpentine, resin, tar (eight dozen), brooms, cotton, ribbons, combs, pins, 'plasters'—and 'tenes balls'. John Hendly died in August 1682. He too was a grocer, and his house in Ash contained four rooms, his shop, a hall, and two chambers, with, outside, a stable where he kept his mare and its saddle and bridle. His stock-in-trade included 56 lb. of sugar (£1 3s.), 56 lb. of cheese (4d. a lb.), 28 lb. of rice (4s. 6d.), a firkin and a half of soap (£1), two 'wey' of cheese (£2 18s.), 56 lb. of 'Chesser' and 56 lb. of 'Warwicke' cheese (£1 2s.), a firkin of butter (15s.), 'half a hundred' of shot (6s.); 'parcels' of salt, meal, tobacco pipes and boxes, currants and 'mopps', and coal, 'a hundred and a ½ of tobacco' (£2), and eight dozen candles (£1 6s.). He only had £1 in ready money, but the 'debts in the shop book' amounted to £4 3s. 1d., and he was owed £30 'on bond'. But at his death in July 1707 Henry Ansley, a butcher in Ash Street with a wife and two children, was in dire financial straits. All he had was valued at only £2 3s. until, three weeks later, his widow Amy received an additional £2 4s. from their landlord, John Wood of Richborough, 'the overplus returned by him to me of what remained of my husband's goods by him distrayned for rent due to him from my said husband at his death, after the rent charges of distress deducted'.

Thomas Young of Goldstone died in September 1666, Joseph Wells of Chequer in August 1667, and Thomas St Nicholas himself in July 1668. All were substantial house-holders. Young's house at Goldstone contained a hall (where he kept a halberd, pike and musket, as well as his fowling-piece), parlour, kitchen, back kitchen, two butteries and their passage, brew-house, milk-house, and bunting-house, and five bed-chambers (including 'the painted chamber', where he stored the best suit of horse harness). He farmed 258 acres, and in his barns when he died was wheat from 140 acres, barley from 55 acres, tares from six acres, horse-beans from 21 acres, and oats from seven acres. There were four loads of hay (besides six more loads at Kingston). His livestock included 16 hogs, two sows with young pigs and 18 'livers', four calves, 22 ducks, 22 geese, 18 turkeys, and 10 hens 'and a few chicken with them'.

Chequer was a smaller house. There, Joseph Wells had a hall, parlour, kitchen and buttery, with only two chambers, his own and the servants', upstairs, and a brew-house, bunting-house, milk-house, and cheese-house, and chaff and wheat lofts. He farmed 142 acres on which, when he died, there were 28 acres of growing wheat, 22 acres of barley and 23 acres of podware and beans. He had a mare and colt, a grey mare, and three geldings (two brown and one sorrel), a bull, six cows, two yearling heifers, a two-year-old steer, and four 12-month-old 'buds', 15 hogs, eight 'liver' pigs, four small pigs and a sow with eight pigs.

The Mote at Hoaden, Thomas St Nicholas' home, was the largest house in Ash. Downstairs there were hall, best parlour, little parlour, kitchen and two butteries (one containing 'An Engine to pull up hoppoles'), a study (with a 'presse of bookes old and new £60'). There were eleven rooms with beds in them (including the 'brushing chamber', the chamber over the clock-house, and the 'chamber within the parlour'), a gallery next to the best chamber with a closet at one end, and a garret. Below, there were two cellars; and, outside, brew-house, milk-house, malt-house (and in it eight bushels of yellow pease), work-house, lodge and stable. St Nicholas owned 74 ounces of silver plate, valued at 5s. an ounce, as well as pewterware weighing 168 pounds, worth 11d. a pound. 'Arms belonging to the house' included a musket, pike, three swords, bandolier and a pair of 'scoch' pistols. There were just two horses in the stable, two cows and two hogs in the yard; 12 sheep and six lambs in the 'Cherry garden', and 'some pears there and before the kitchen door'. He was the owner of 146 acres of land, but perhaps occupied little of it himself. When he died he had an acre of hops, some hemp and two acres of wheat 'on the ground', some more wheat, peas and beans and 'small seeds', and 'two nurseries of young trees' in Hoden Field. He was also entitled to some 'fruit & cropp upon ye ground the halfe part', presumably shared with the occupier, instead of charging rent. He was owed £1 5s. for cherries, £6 for rent due from the 'small tenants', and another £40 7s. in 'debts speratt'—and £1,300 in 'desperate debts'.

The Royalist Thomas Peke of Hills Court died in December 1677, when his wearing apparel and ready money were estimated at £35, rent due to him at £90, and 'debts desperate' at £42. In the house were an 'old' parlour, a 'new' parlour, a 'little' parlour, kitchen, butteries and cellar, four chambers (including the 'red chamber' with its 'old red hangings' and his 'Library of Books' (£35)), lumber room and garret. Several rooms had hangings, and window curtains and rods. In the old parlour were stored a wheel for spinning linen, and 'A Troopeing Saddle & Furniture belonging to a Troope horse with Pistolls & sword & Coat' (together valued at £3 10s.). Outside were a brew-house, milk-house, old lumber loft and a barn. He owned 100 acres of land but, apart from his coach, two horses and their harness (together, £25), his only livestock were two fat hogs; and he had only small quantities of wheat and other corn and 'small beans'.

Daniel Nott, who occupied 70 acres at Cop Street, died in February 1682. His farmhouse consisted of hall, parlour and kitchen, three chambers and a garret, stable and two barns. In the yard were eight cows, two heifers, 12 yearling 'bodes', 4 hogs and 10 pigs; in the stable, five horses and two colts; and out in the pasture, 25 sheep and 19 lambs. In one barn were 37 quarters and two bushels of wheat, barley in the 'toss', and 'beanes threshed and unthreshed'; and in the other three quarters and one bushel of beans, some 'Turkey beans', and some flax and flax seed. In June 1682, John Laighill, who farmed 137 acres at Lowton south of Richborough, died. His home was modest: a parlour, kitchen with a small room next to it, and a single chamber; and outside, stable, lodges, barn and granary, but he owned 'several sorts of books' (£5 10s.) as well as a fowling-piece, two muskets and a sword and belt. In the meadow and on the marshes he had a bull, 10 cows, three heifers, three 12-month-old 'buds' and three weaning calves, two mares and a 'sucking colt', two geldings and three gelding colts, 17 ewes and 12 lambs, and six hogs and sows. In his barn were 29 quarters of wheat and nine bushels of small beans. It was summer and he had growing crops: 34 acres of wheat, 12 acres of barley, 15 acres of 'pease of all sorts', nine acres of garden beans, six acres of grey peas and tares, and two acres of canary seed. He had £20 in ready money when he died, and had lent money extensively 'In bonds and writings concerning money due amounting in all to the sum of debts some desperate £339 9s. 1d.'; he also had £20 invested 'In shipping'. Also in June 1682, Stephen Solly of Wingham Barton died, leaving a widow, Mercy, who survived him by only three years. Their house contained a hall (in which were a musket and fowling-piece), parlour, kitchen, six chambers (including the 'apple

28 School Farmhouse at Guilton, dated 1691, with true 'Dutch' gables. Given in 1721 by the Cartwright sisters to trustees as an endowment for the village charity school, the farm was sold about 1947.

chamber' where dressed hemp, peas, apples and pears were in store), a 'beer buttery', another buttery, coal-house, and milk-house. Outside there were a stable, granary, and 'podder' and wheat barns. He too was owed £20 on bond, 'supposed desperate'. He, and she after him, owned a one-sixteenth share in two hoys: *The Adventure* of which George Hurst was master, and another of which Thomas Young was master. As well as 171 acres at Wingham Barton, they occupied other land at Ware. When he died, 35 quarters of his wheat had been 'sent to London' and sold at 25s., two more quarters were in the barn still to thresh, and 'some beans in a house in Sandwich'. There were still 47 acres of growing wheat, 21 acres of barley, 20 acres of beans, seven acres of flax, seven acres of yellow peas, about 18 acres of 'grey Pease greate & small with a few Tares', and half an acre of hemp. He had five mares and three geldings, 10 milking cows, a young bull, and five 12-month-old cattle, 10 'great hogs of all sorts', 17 'liver' hogs, and small pigs, and, on the marsh, some fatting cattle (a bull, four cows, four heifers, and four steers).

When Thomas Baker died in September 1687, his farmhouse at Guston had just a hall, parlour and kitchen, with two chambers above them; but it also had a milk-house, small beer buttery, quern house (and loft over), and 'sink house', as well as a granary, stable and barn. His wheat, barley, and great and small beans, were all still unthreshed, as well as 'poder that is peas and tares and oats', and some apples were still on the trees (12s.). In his stable were five geldings, a mare and a yearling mare colt; in the yard, five great hogs and two sows and 20 'livers'; on the marsh, 11 milking cows, 17 barren sheep, 14 'rom' lambs and 17 yearling wethers, and at 'the Rood House' two bulls, four fat heifers and six weaning calves.

Francis Wood did not long survive the affair with Love. He died in October 1697. He farmed 273 acres at Richborough, living in a modest farmhouse: hall, parlour, and kitchen, with three chambers above, milk-house and brew-house, and separate cellars for strong beer and small beer. In the stable he kept a riding mare, two mares and two geldings, four second team horses (three geldings and a mare), four colts and a blind gelding. In the yard were 16 great hogs, 20 'sheats', three sows and a boar, four steers, two fatting heifers, two young heifers, and 10 calves, and five ewes and seven lambs. In the barns were wheat 'threshed and unthreshed', barley (some in stack, some still uncarried), oats, great beans, small beans, yellow peas, grey peas and hay. He had £15 in ready money; and he too had lent money, seemingly very prudently: his 'debts recoverable' totalled £110, his 'debts desperate' only £15. He also was involved in 'Adventures at Sea': he had a thirty-second share in two ships; the *John and Mary* (master Samuel Ferrier) and the *Abigail* (Maris Atkins), and a sixteenth share in five more: a 'wessell' (master Richard Castle), a 'pinke' (master Roger Tisdall), and three hoys (masters Thomas Jennings, John Cousser and John Sutton), all valued together at £156.

In August 1709, Jeffery Foat, the tenant of Goshall, 'strangled himself', leaving a widow and three children. His troubles cannot have been financial, for he was prosperous enough, paying £147 a year in rent for his 230-acre farm, and leaving personal estate valued at £790. The house had a hall, parlour, four chambers, a closet (in which hemp was stored), wheat, apple, bean and wool lofts above, a cellar below (which contained '11 beer casks with beer in them and six dozen bottles'), a milk-house, brew-house, and bunting-house. In 1705 he had had three servants 'living-in': Edward White, 'his mate' John Goodbone, and Elizabeth Bing. Now, outside, was the year's harvest: 78 quarters of wheat (valued at £157), 78 quarters of barley (£73 19s.), 132½ quarters of beans (£98 17s. 6d.), some peas (£17 10s.), and fruit (10s.). On the farm there were four geldings, four mares and a sucking colt; a bull, 11 milking cows, 11 heifers, four bullocks, two steers, a bull steer, five 'runts' and two calves, 61 sheep and nine lambs, 11 hogs, six 'livers' and 12 pigs.

NINE

EIGHTEENTH-CENTURY ASH

Shocklidge was succeeded in 1713 as the archishop's 'perpetual curate', by Obadiah Bourne, a young man of 28 from a Derbyshire clerical family. The vicar of Margate described him to Archbishop Wake in 1716 as 'allied to the sons of Eli', clearly not intended as praise, though it is to be hoped that the description was not exact. ('The sons of Eli were sons of Belial; they knew not the Lord ... they lay with the women that assembled at the door of the tabernacle of the congregation' (1 Samuel 2, xii and xxii)) He was also appointed curate of Goodnestone the next year, but resigned both curacies and returned to a family living in Derbyshire in 1721.

Then followed two perpetual curates each of whom served the parish for thirty years or more until their deaths: Francis Conduit from 1721 until 1753, and Benjamin Longley from 1753 until 1783. Both lived at Ash, although both held other preferments: Conduit was rector of Snave from 1738; Longley vicar of Tong and Eynsford from 1750. Both of them were buried at Ash. Neither seems to have left much mark for posterity.

29   Guilton sandpit, from the south, 1854, showing that three windmills still existed there then. From *Inventorium Sepulchrale* ed. Charles Roach Smith, 1856; the artist is unknown.

30 Mount Ephraim mill, seen here *c.*1935: a post-mill, originally erected in 1735 at Ringleton, and re-erected at Ash in 1818. It had two cloth-covered sweeps, commons, and two shuttered sweeps. Until it blew over in a gale in October 1955 and was wrecked, it was the oldest surviving mill in Kent.

Longley, a bachelor, made his will in August 1781, eighteen months before his death. After expressing his gratitude to his sister Frances Longley 'for her care of me', he referred less warmly to another sister, Elizabeth Longley, who 'has lived with me for 20 years, and has not as yet paid anything for her board'.

In 1721 Eleanor and Anne Cartwright 'beautified and adorned' the chancel of the church. In 1727 the churchwardens bought a new font of marble: perhaps the old one had been damaged in its travels. It was evidently something of an occasion, too, when in June 1741 'ye Young people were Confirmed about 150 in Number and Upwards of 60 Parishnrs was there on Horseback'. But the fabric of the church required increasing expenditure by the churchwardens. They had had partially to rebuild the south transept in 1675, when perhaps they also demolished the south aisle. In 1736 they took down and rebuilt the spire, and re-leaded the roof of the tower (a job they had to repeat in 1771). In 1779 they contracted with Thomas Swain for the re-casting of the five bells and the addition of three more, at a cost of over £250. That was not money well spent, for in 1791, only 12 years later, they had to have all eight re-cast by Mears & Stainbank in Whitechapel.

In 1738 a furious row erupted over the ownership of a pew in the church. In 1690 Lady Wilde of Goldstone had been granted a faculty to erect a pew (11 feet long, seven feet broad, and about five feet in height, containing two seats) in the chancel. Shortly afterwards, she had 'left off frequenting the church, being a non-juror'. The chancel was the responsibility of the archbishops, and so reckoned to belong to their lessees at Guilton parsonage. The pew, 'a large square pew with a servants pew contiguous and adjoining the back of it', was one of two in the chancel (the other being used by the curate and his family), and had been occupied by successive lessees of the parsonage: by the Cartwrights (in company with Lady Wilde's daughter-in-law, Margaret Wilde), by Mrs. Susan Roberts, and (since 1733) by Mrs. Roberts' daughter Catherine and son-in-law, John Finney, D.D. In 1737 Finney left Ash to visit his own Devonshire parish. When he returned the following year he found that Lady Wilde's granddaughter Margaret Masters and her husband John had moved from their own pew in the nave, and taken possession of this one. They refused Finney admission to it. He in turn locked it to exclude them, and began a suit in the Canterbury Consistory Court, claiming 'perturbation of seat'. He was determined not to compromise: 'You may depend upon it I shall come to no accommodation with Masters unless he quits all claim to the Pew and pays our full costs'. Several parishioners gave evidence about the history of the pew. Finally, in January 1742, the Court decided that Lady Wilde's faculty had been granted irregularly by the Dean and Chapter of Canterbury in 1690 during the vacancy in the see caused by Archbishop Sancroft's deprivation, and so was void. The Masters were ordered not to use the pew, and to pay the costs of the suit.

After their victory at Fontenoy in 1745, during the War of Austrian Succession, the French overran nearly all Flanders. Worse, the English army had to withdraw across the Channel to deal with the Jacobite rising in Scotland. At Ash, Finney preached a sermon, afterwards printed, 'On the occasion of the designed Invasion of the French when the general call was to meet armed on Barham Downs'. In February 1749, the churchwardens 'pd ye Fiddlers when Peace was proclaim'd 3. 0.' But in 1755 soldiers were quartered in Ash, at the *Ship*, the *Chequer*, the *Duke*, the *George*, the *Red Lion*, and the *Bull's Head*. The register entry for Isaac Pay's burial on 2 July 1758 noted that he had been 'run over by a waggon'.

In 1772 the archdeacon ordered the churchwardens to see that the Molland chancel was repaired. This was the responsibility of the owner of Molland, which had been bought by William Allen, a Canterbury brewer, in 1753. (In April 1758 Allen had given John Masters leave to bury his wife Margaret in the Molland chancel, and to be buried there himself.) About 1765 Allen had re-tiled the roof but, unable to agree on the price for ceiling it—Henry Bransford had asked 15d. a square yard, and Allen had been unwilling to pay more than 12d.—nothing had been done. After Allen died in 1772, his widow still failed to repair it and, at last, in 1779 the churchwardens brought a suit against her in the Court of Arches, the archbishops' provincial court, complaining that the chancel was now

> in a very ruinous, decayed, dilapidated condition, and particularly in the Roof Tyling Walls windows and pavement thereof, which were and are so much dilapidated and out of repair that the congregation who attend to hear divine service & sermons in the parish church of Ash are greatly annoyed by the wind, snow and rain which enter at the roof and windows, and cannot in comfort attend their devotions.

The Dean of Arches ordered her to repair it at once, and to pay the churchwardens' costs of the case.

In March 1797 Nehemiah Nisbett, the curate, preached and published a sermon on 'Ezekiel's warning to the Jews, applied to the threatened invasion of Great Britain'. In October, Citizen-General Bonaparte was appointed to command the French 'Army of England', and, in the spring of 1798, a French invasion was daily expected. A great military encampment was set up on the Downs between Canterbury and Deal, and William Pitt, the prime minister, took up residence at Walmer Castle. Out of patriotism—or to avoid the annual militia ballot—many joined the Volunteers. In February, 297 men of Ash agreed to serve with the Sandwich Volunteers, assembling at the *Ship Inn*; four on horseback (one with both sword and pike), others on foot with firelocks or pikes, others as labourers with axes, pickaxes or spades, or as servants with cattle or teams of horses. With 74 men from Woodnesborough, 42 from Staple and 24 from Elmstone, they

31 Royal Arms of George III (including the short-lived Electoral bonnet of Hanover), 1810, in St Nicholas Church. The Royal Arms of 1660 were, with due parish economy, re-used as the backing, and only came to light again in the 1980s.

pledged themselves to 'unite as one Man in offering our assistance either to oppose, repel and Destroy the Enemy or to Guard and Protect the Women, Children, Aged & Infirm ... in such manner as may render to our King & Country the most effectual service.'

In 1803, invasion seemed imminent. Listing possible French landing places, Admiral Lord Keith said, 'I think the Downs are secure unless the Enemy be superior by sea, and that Pegwell Bay is too difficult ... and is protected by being in the immediate vicinity of the Downs'. In November 1804, the Vestry granted John Scarlett, the overseer, a rate of 6d. 'for the purpose of defraying the expences respecting the Military Forces'. In that year the Duke of York wanted to place a Martello tower 'at the entrance to the Sandwich river'; in the end 73 were built, but none in Pegwell Bay. Without a fleet to escort them after Trafalgar, the invasion barges never sailed out of Boulogne. Had they done so, Napoleon said afterwards, their 'real point of landing would have been somewhere between Deal and Margate'.

In 1813 England was still battling to defeat Napoleon, and every available soldier was being sent to join Wellington's army in Spain. On the road from Canterbury through Ash these were stirring times, and the *Kentish Gazette* reported

> The lines of road leading to our City and the coast have been occupied with the movement of troops. The men from Chatham ... arrived on Wednesday at Deal and were embarked on the men-of-war in the Downs. Another detachment of the same corps were conveyed into this city this morning by waggons and in the late afternoon continued ... to Deal. At the same time the Royal Marine Artillery, consisting of six 9-pounders and one howitzer, also arrived from Chatham, each gun drawn by 4 packhorses, and passed through at full gallop for the same destination.

Ten

The Vestry and the Poor
'The absence of common courtesy'

In 1705 there were 1,191 inhabitants of the parish living in 268 households (a striking increase on the 106 of the 1664 Hearth Tax return, so Benchkin's estimate of 220 in 1677 may not have been so far out). Poor relief was regularly paid to 39 households, in which 60 adults (21 married couples and 18 widows) and 70 children (in 26 of those households) lived.

The Vestry met monthly to conduct its business, sometimes in the chancel of the church, sometimes in the school loft, but usually at one or other of the village inns. Nearly always it was mostly concerned with the care of the parish poor.

December 29th 1709: At a Vestery held at the Ship Was Orderd as followeth

Order'd Stephen Sanders Sen 2 shilling p week. Order'd that Soll: Sturges have a Coat as soon as Conveniently it may be. Order'd that Robt Minter take the Boy that is at Mr Smalls Prentice untill he be twenty years old and the Pish to pay him £15; that is £5 p. year for the first 3 years and that the Pish find him Cloaths at the time of his taking him fiting for an aprentice, and the said Robt Minter to find him Cloath ye time of his Aprenticeship and also Shall Release him, Suffcently well Cloath'd at the end of the said Term. Order'd that the Pish pay Edward Anslow rent no Longer but till Ladyday Next. Order'd Step Danton Half a Load of Wood.

January the 26th 1710 at a vestery held at the Lion Was Ordered as followeth

Ordered to Pay 15s. for John Knight Toward the payment of his Rent. Ordered to allow John Jull tenn shillings to by him some Leather, and two shilling more to by him Tools. Ordered to allow the Wid Price 1s. 6d. p. week. Ordered that Goody Tilly have 4 Pair of Shoes for her Children.

March ye 30th 1710 At a Vestery held at John Beales it was Order'd as followeth

Order'd that Goody Smiths Daughter hav a payer of Shoes two changes and a Coat. Order'd that John Knight have ½ a Load of Wood and that he be Relieved in Extraordinarys at ye Overseers Desretion. Order'd that Stephen Dantons girle that Lives at Goodman Keels have a gown. Order'd that Stephen Walker have two Coats and a payer of Breetches for his Boys. Order'd that John Fennells Jun his Wife have 6d. p week added to her pay. Order'd that there be paid for Henry Reely half a years rent: £1 10s.

In 1710 there was smallpox in Ash, and many children died. The overseers helped the families of the sick: 'p^d Two Woemen for watching with Fennells children 1s.'; and with the expense of laying out those who died: 'p^d Deborah Solly for watching with and laying forth of Fennells child 2s. 6d. p^d Deborah Solly for laying forth another Fennells children 2s.' Paupers' funeral expenses, including beer for the mourners, were paid as a matter of course. Again, in 1747, 13 families were granted relief because their children had smallpox. Help was also given when children caught measles. Sometimes the parish acted to head off future expense; in 1713 the overseers gave 2s. to 'a wench that has a great belly to get her clear of the Parish', and in 1732 sent two women to London 'to be cured of the Itch and the Venereal disease'.

When in 1678 Goody Wheeler was 'removed' to Ash, her place of settlement, without any possessions, the overseers spent 3s. 6d. buying for her 'A paire of old Bellowes and An old White Blankett and a Chaff bolster and a Canstick And a pillow and potthangers and some old potts and crockes'.

But when Henry Young died in 1712 he had been receiving poor relief, so the parish sold his bed and distributed his clothes among his relations and other poor people:

> To John Young ye sheets, Peter Young one waistcoat, Stephen Lacy one payer of breeches, Lawrence Cater one jacket, Lawrence Palmer one jacket, John Riens one shift, Goody Grant one coat, one shift, one payer of stockings, Robert Barows one payer of breeches, Henry Palmer one more jacket.

The parish officers came under increasing pressure to contain the growing cost of keeping the poor in house-rent, firewood and clothing and of paying them weekly allowances. In 1725 the Vestry agreed that the churchwardens and overseer 'do build or hire at ye charge of ye Parish a house for the use of ye Poor'. They leased a house in The Street, opposite the church, from John Bax, and the Vestry contracted to pay Henry Eastman and his wife

> ten pounds per Annum and Alsoe meat drink and Lodging for Looking after ye poor of the Parish of Ash for Seven Years; provided that ye sd Henry Eastman and his wife take care the poor be well Look't after and kept to work as the Officers and ye Major part of ye Parishnrs shall think Convenient.

But what lay behind the decision in 1730 that 'Joseph Horn is to have ye workhouse cow for ye sum of three pounds three shillings'?

In the 1660s Dr. Carder had been paid £4 'for all cures made by him for the poor of Ash', and further similar agreements followed. Dr. Hayward was paid for his attention to a wound 'received by horses running away with Harrows at Mr. Woods of Richborough'. In 1730 Dr. Hogben agreed that he would

> look after all the poor in ye Workhouse and all that Receive Weekly Collection for ye sum of ten pounds per Year Except Broken Bones & what ye Overseer shall think fit to send him to which have not Weekly Collection, and for them he is to be paid as ye Overseer and he shall agree for, and in Case ye Small pox should be reef for ye sd Docr to be allow'd a Reasonable Allowance.

In 1731 the Vestry entered into two agreements with Thomas Cusins: first, in May, it agreed, as it commonly did in such cases

> that Tho: Cusons take Ann Chandler from this time to Easter Next on Condition ye s^d Ann Chandler like of her service, and the Parish to Cloathe her, and ye s^d Tho: Cossens is to find ye s^d Ann Chandler in Meat Drink Washing and Lodging during ye time and to keep her Mended,

and then, in December,

> to pay to Tho: Cusins the sum of one pound ten shillings for Ringing ye Bell at four a clock in the Morning nd Eight at Night Constantly from Michaelmas Day to Ladyday, and the Money to be p^d out of the poor Sess,

so Cusins himself was not above getting out of bed early.

In 1780 the Vestry built a new workhouse, 'large and commodious', on the Sandwich road. It agreed to pay John Hendrix and his wife Silvester £15 per annum 'for their care and trouble as Master and Mistress of the Workhouse', that their two children aged 8 and 5 should be provided for in the workhouse as other children were (clothing excepted), and that 'as the younger child becomes capable of being Imploy'd in the Work done in the House, the Parish Agree to Increase the salary agreeable to what he may be supposed to earn and when he is judged to be capable of earning his living the salary to be increased to £20 p.a.' Evidently the eight-year-old was already considered as earning his living.

The Vestry also agreed 'not to allow any persons anything weekly out of the house nor to pay any rents for any houses from the 10th October next'. In the following year it was agreed that the surgeon John Surrage should 'look after the Poor this Year ensuing for £20 per Ann for the People in the House and others that the Overseer shall think proper'. At Easter 1783 John Scarlett was appointed overseer, a position he held until 1815.

The population of the parish increased from 1,191 in 1705 to 1,575 in 1801 (32 per cent), and to 1,685 in 1811 (7 per cent). Thereafter it continued to rise rapidly, to 2,021 in 1821 (20 per cent), and 2,140 in 1831 (6 per cent). (It did not reach that figure again until 1881.)

In 1779 Edward Hasted noted that in Ash the number of poor 'constantly relieved' was about 75, and 'casually' 55, at an annual cost of £1,000—which he contrasted with the £29 15s. 11d. spent in Ash on poor relief in 1604. Although the parish poor rate held steady for 20 years, averaging 1s. 9d. in the pound between 1780 and 1799, it then began to rise steadily, to an average of 2s. 9d. between 1800 and 1809 (excluding a special rate of 6d. in 1804 'for defraying the Expences respecting the Military Forces'), and 3s. 3d. for the seven

32 Cottages in Goodban Square (drawn by Fred Adcock, c.1920). They were rented by the Ash Vestry as the parish poorhouse in 1725.

years 1810-16. The fall in agricultural prices after the peace of 1815 and the rising population resulted in higher unemployment. In 1816 John Boys commented that the condition of the poor was 'worse than ever known'. The poor rate in Ash suddenly more than doubled, to 7s. 6d. in 1817, and 8s. 6d. in 1818. It was never quite so high again, but still averaged 4s. 6d. for 1820-9, and 5s. 5d. for 1830-5. In 1817 the number of poor households regularly receiving weekly relief was 99, including 31 widows.

As the burden of the poor rate increased, the overseers tried harder to save money, and the plight of the poor became more desperate. When a poor person became (or, until 1795, even looked as if he *might* become) dependent on parish relief, and had no legal 'settlement' by birth or employment in the parish, parish officers would have him 'removed' to whatever parish he was legally settled in. Of 171 removal orders obtained by the Ash overseers, 49 were made between 1765 and 1798, and 101 between 1799 and 1818—and 95 dated from a single year, 1807. It was two-way traffic. Thomas Turner, probably as a young man in the 1790s, lived in Ash for about five years, first as a waggoner to Mr. Minter, and then as a 'looker', managing water levels and grazing stock on the Ash Level, living in a cottage with a small garden for which he paid a rent of £7 a year. To supplement his income he hired a cow from one man for £1 11s. 6d. a year, and its keep from another at 1s. 6d. a week, on the basis that he had the milk and butter from the cow but that its calf was the property of the cow's owner. But this arrangement came to an end, and Turner moved to Sandwich, where his wife died, his two elder children went into service, and the two younger into the poorhouse. He then moved again, to Sittingbourne, and remarried. In 1817, aged 47, he could get no work, and applied to the overseers there for help. They appealed to the magistrates, who decided that because when in Ash he had paid more than £10 a year in rent (counting what he paid for the cow) his 'settlement' was in Ash, and removed him back here. His wife seems not to have come with him, and after two years on weekly relief at Ash, he probably went into the workhouse, where he died 25 years later.

Not surprisingly, rural society seemed to be becoming more lawless. An Association for the Protection of Property of the United Parishes of Ash, Preston, Stourmouth and Elmstone was meeting at the *Ship* by 1809. In 1814 James Harlow of Ash was convicted 'for having in his possession a hare which had been shot, and fined the sum of £5, being the mitigated penalty for that offence ... half of which sum was given to the informer and the remainder for the poor of the parish'. In the same year, the churchwardens paid out 6s. 8d. 'for Advertising the Church Robbery'. On 28 March 1817 the *Kentish Gazette* advertised

FIFTEEN POUNDS REWARD

Whereas on Saturday Night last, or early on Sunday morning, some person or persons forcibly broke open and entered the Round-house, or Storehouse, attached to the Mill situate on Mount Ephraim, in the parish of Ash, next Sandwich, belonging to Mr Zechariah Hudson, and stole therefrom Three Bushels and a half, or thereabouts, of MEAL, with the sack. A Reward of TEN POUNDS is hereby offered for the apprehension of the offender or offenders, over and above a reward of FIVE POUNDS, offered by the Society for the prosecution of Thieves and Felons, to be paid on conviction.

ZECHARIAH HUDSON.

Less than two months later, there appeared another notice:

Whereas Good Intent Mill in the parish of Ash next Sandwich, belonging to Messrs Kelsey and Company, was forcibly broke into on Tuesday night or early on Wednesday morning last, and two sacks containing about four bushels of wholemeal in each sack, stolen and carried away by some person or persons from out of the said mill. For the apprehension of any one, or more, concerned in the aforesaid robbery, a reward of ten pounds is hereby offered, over and above the reward allowed by the Association, to be paid on conviction, by applying to George Culmer, Secretary to the Association.

Preston, May 15th, 1817.

The Vestry continued to make 'bulk' agreements with doctors. In 1810 it was noted

that Mr. Spencer undertakes to attend the Paupers [as] well within as without the Parish within five Miles from the Church, by a written order from a parish officer, including Fractures, Midwifery, and everything belonging to the Medical business (Inoculation only excepted) for the sum of Fifty Pounds per Annum.

33 Mount Pleasant Row in Sandwich Road, c.1875. The nine cottages had been built by the Ash Vestry in 1822 to house some of the parish poor. Their neat cobbled frontage contrasted with the mud of the carriageway. This is one of several photographs of Ash taken about 1875, probably all by William Henry Boyer (1827-97) of Sandwich.

But in 1817 it agreed with him that 'in consideration of the great increase in Paupers
… in the case of Midwifery the number exceeding Fifteen Women shall be paid at One
Guinea each'.

In that year the Vestry tried to reduce the cost to the ratepayers by requiring each
farmer to employ more men. It was agreed

> that any Parishioner working a Team, should constantly imploy Two labourers belonging to the
> Parish, and so in proportion to any Number of Horses kept by them … The number above
> named to be kept in constant employ or paid for by the Defaulters to the Overseer. If any
> Gentleman should not have his full Number of Men, to give notice in Writing of the Number
> of Men wanted by him at the Poor House on Thursday morning, which Men will be sent on
> Friday Morning to their work. The Men will be drawn by Ballot and sent accordingly when
> wanted. It was also Agreed that the Poor of the House should be sent to work to any Parishioner
> offering the best Price per Day, such offer to be sent to the Poor House in writing directed
> to the Overseer on Thursday morning or on Personal Application to the Committee.

In order to modernise the working arrangements in the workhouse and increase the
accommodation there, in 1817 the Vestry also agreed

> to remove the Looms of the Weaving Trade at the Poor House to the Warehouse, repairing
> the same, and inclosing the Dutch Barn for a Spinning Shop and, for the better convenience
> of the Poor of the House, to fit up a Room for certain Families, converting the Weaving Shop
> to Sleeping Rooms, building a Coal Hole, and making a Double Door at the Entrance of the
> Workhouse.

The parish officers agreed to borrow £600 for the purpose, and to pay interest at 5 per
cent.

> Wishing to act with equity, that no censure or misunderstanding shall or may arise in the minds
> of the Parishioners hereafter as to their conduct, they do fully consider the Stock and Debt
> of the Trade on the Average to be fully equal to the above Principal sum of Six hundred
> pounds …

and added that they did 'consider the building and repairing the said premises highly
necessary and advantageous to the Parish'.

In 1819 the Vestry agreed 'to build seven cottages at the Upper End of the Poor
House Garden adjoining the New Street Road'. (The seven cottages were still there, all
owner-occupied, in 1999.)

In March 1822 the Vestry decided to contract for the supply of the poor with 'good
wheaten bread'; that the poor should be paid at the rate of 6s. for a man and his wife;
that a couple with children should also have 6lb of bread for each child; and that 'for
the further encouragement of Industry, every labourer shall be furnished with Bread at
the Contract price, not exceeding six pounds per Week for Each Member of the Family'.

In September 1822 the Vestry advertised in the *Kentish Gazette* for a contractor
willing 'to victual and clothe the Poor in the Workhouse at per head per week', and
accepted James Goldsmith's tender to do so for 2s. 10d. It was also decided to share out
the services of the unemployed among ratepayers according to the rateable value of their
property, the parish paying the men for their labour.

The labourers out of employ shall be distributed among the several Occupiers for employment within the Parish, as a Parish or Roundsman, being paid for their labour by the Overseers, upon the following plan: For every Four pounds rental as per ad valorem of the Parish, one day's labour from one man; That the services of such Parish or Roundsman may be accepted or rejected, in the whole or in part, at the option of the occupiers; That such Parish or Roundsman shall not be allowed to perform the undermentioned work: Thrashing or with Thrashing machines; Turning or spreading manure; Carting manure from Mixens; With the Horses, Ploughing, Harrowing, etc.; Sowing Corn or with Drill Machines; Hoeing Corn; Digging, Cutting and Poling Hops; Pulling, Stripping and Stacking Poles. Should any be desired to perform any such labour then to be entitled to a full rate of pay, and paid accordingly by the Party so employing them. That there shall be no selection of labourers. That the appointment of labour shall be Five days in each week, commencing on Friday and ending on Wednesday. That each Labourer shall be desired to call upon every occupier or occupiers for whom he may be allotted to work during the ensuing week on or before 3 o'clock on Thursday afternoon to apprise him or them of such allotment and for directions what to do, or should the service or services not be required, that the same may be known. That every occupier must require the labourers to be punctual in their time, in going to and on leaving work, also that they be industrious while at work. That every occupier must send the Overseer an account weekly, of the number of days' work performed by each labourer, such account being a voucher for payment by the Overseer. That no occupier shall be entitled to a second portion of labour until each shall have had their full allotment, or the option thereof, according to the several Rentals throughout the Parish.

In 1824 it was agreed to pay Goldsmith an additional 4d. per head per week whenever the average price of a quarter of wheat reached 55s. or more. The Vestry again shared the unemployed out among the occupiers, but now on an acreage basis, and with the employers paying the men but receiving a 'premium' or subsidy from the parish agreed in respect of each individual man. This was the arrangement referred to by Henry Boyce, of Waldershare, when he told a Parliamentary Committee in 1828 that 'In the parish of Ash, there is a regular meeting every Thursday, and the paupers are put up to auction. The best will fetch the full pay of twelve shillings a week … If a person bids eight or ten, it is made up by the poor rates.' The parish retained this system right up until 1834, although not without annual, and evidently sometimes heated, discussion. The Vestry assumed direct management of the Poor House and of 'the Manufactory' in 1828. At Michaelmas 1829 it took on a tenancy of School Farm at Guilton 'so that the Overseer may employ the Paupers of the Parish rather than have them kept in idleness'.

In December 1829 the Kent Grand Jury was so concerned by 'the deep and unprecedented distress which … prevails among all classes throughout this county' that it petitioned the prime minister, the Duke of Wellington.

The Ash overseer in 1830, Michael Becker of Upper Goldstone Farm, was a hard man. The curate, George Gleig, said that Becker compelled single men to enter the workhouse 'whence they were marched out every day in gangs … If no better employment could be found for able-bodied paupers, he caused them to dig holes in the ground, and fill them up again'. When John Fordred, an Ash shepherd with a wife and five children, honest and industrious but with no work, and living at Margate, applied for relief, Becker granted him 9s. a week—but made him walk to Ash every day except

Sunday for his 18d. After Fordred had walked 26 miles a day for nine weeks, on what food he could get from his share of the 9s., his strength gave out.

In that year, threshing-machine breaking began in Kent, and spread across southern England. Long afterwards, Gleig told how he and his churchwarden, 'good George Quested' of Chequer, had

> trotted down to ... Westmarsh and encountered a body of 40 or 50 men who had just smashed a threshing-machine at one farmhouse, and were moving towards another ... The rioters agreed to follow me quietly into the village ... Once, ... coming on a threshing-machine ... a partial rush was made towards it. But when I dismounted and planted myself beside it, saying ... that I would mark the first man who laid a hand upon it, a shout was raised to 'Let it alone'.

But machines were broken at Richard Southee's farm at Goldstone Court, and at William Petley's at Overland. Later, in October, the rioters turned to stack-burning. The leader of the Ash discontents was known as 'Captain Revell'. After large bodies of men had been seen 'marching with bludgeons on the roads near Ash', Becker's stackyard at Upper Goldstone was gutted by fire, perhaps in vengeance, but no charges were ever brought. By mid-November the 7th Dragoon Guards had been posted to Canterbury to restore order.

In Kent, 77 rioters were convicted. Of five—all found guilty of arson—who were sentenced to death, four were hanged; 25 more were transported (23 to Van Diemen's Land, and two to New South Wales), and 48 imprisoned. For their part in the affair at Goldstone Court, John Stannard and William Stone were both transported for seven years, and two others given terms of imprisonment; and two more were imprisoned for the breaking at Overland. The rioters went on from Ash to Stourmouth and Wingham and, for similar offences there, Thomas Reed (who had a previous conviction for theft) was transported for life, and William Strood and Harry Andrews for seven years. Probably all but Reed were pardoned in 1835, and Reed in 1836. None is known to have returned to England. At least one, Stannard, became a farmer in Van Diemen's Land.

Gleig believed the riots were the result of 'distress arising from low and unfair wages and, in some degree, the absence of common courtesy in the farmer towards his labourer'. He looked back with nostalgia to the Napoleonic wars: 'During the good times of war, when the demand for labour was great, working men received ... half a crown a day, ... wheat sold for ninety or a hundred shillings a quarter, ... working people throve and were contented'. In May 1832, there were 47 inmates of the Ash workhouse, ranging in age from 12 months to 90 years; and 65 of the 344 labourers in the parish were receiving outdoor relief. When a new master left in 1832, it was decided once again 'to farm the poor in the Workhouse, and to advertise for a proper man and his wife to undertake it—"The person so contracting will have the manufactory, with the trade, and the labour of the poor in the workhouse"', and to sell the parish's stock of manufactured goods. This 'Valuable stock of Sacks, Hop Pockets and Bags, Linen, etc.', sold by auction on the premises on Friday, 13 July 1832, comprised 'upwards of 700 quarters of flour and corn sacks, 1,000 hop pockets and bags, several quarters of sacks and bags of other description, a large quantity of very excellent sheeting, towelling, table cloths, canvas, mill-sail ditto, carpeting, door matts, bed sacking, cord, twine, etc.'. In March 1833 the Vestry further refined its scheme for employing men not in the workhouse:

The Paupers shall be employed according to the following scales: 1. A married man without children to be employed three days and a half in a week at the rate of 2s. per day. 2. For every child one half day's work over and above at the rate of one shilling for such portion of the day. 3. The utmost extent of Parish allowance to be 12s. per week.

And in January 1834 the Vestry tried again:

1. That for the space of six months from this date each occupier of land shall employ as regular labourers one man for every thirty acres of arable land in his occupation. 2. That every occupier of Marsh and meadow land shall employ one man for every portion of such land, varying from sixty to one hundred and twenty acres. 3. That the occupier of Tythes shall employ one man for each £150 of rental as assessed for the parochial rates. 4. That the surplus labourers be distributed by the Overseer among the different occupiers in proportion to their rental and be paid by the said overseer according to a fixed scale. 5. That such surplus labourers shall not be transferred by one occupier to another. 6. That all portions of Grass land under sixty acres be class'd for the employment of labourers.

In November it was agreed 'That every occupier of land who shall dig one or more Acres of Arable or Pasture land for the sake of employing the superfluous laborers shall be paid one half of the cost thereof by the Overseer.'

The Poor Law Amendment Act 1834, intended to correct 'the wretched system of our late Poor Laws which … has depraved the labourer and almost ruined the farmer', led to the creation of the Eastry Union and its Board of Guardians, so that from 1836 the Ash Vestry was no longer responsible for the care of the Ash poor. The Vestry decided to give up the tenancy of the Cartwright's School Farm at Michaelmas 1835.

In June 1835 it met 'to consider the policy of enabling one or more Families to Emigrate to Canada', and agreed 'to assist Thomas Pettman & Family to Emigrate to Canada at an expense not exceeding £40' and, in the following March, 'That William Redwood, his Wife and Family, and any other Families that may wish to Emigrate to Canada shall be supplied with Funds for that purpose'. A meeting was convened for 4 April 1836 for the purpose of

considering whether any and what sum not exceeding half the average yearly poor rate for three years now last past shall be raised or borrowed as a fund for defraying the expences of Emigration of poor persons having settlement in the parish and being willing to Emigrate; and for giving directions for raising or borrowing such sum or sums to be paid out of or charged upon the rates raised or to be raised for the relief of the poor of this parish and to be applied under and according to such rules and regulations as the Poor Law Commissioners for England and Wales shall in that behalf direct.

The meeting was twice adjourned, but the Vestry minute book does not reveal whether any or what decision was taken.

In August 1836 the Vestry consented to the sale by the Eastry Board of Guardians of the parish 'Poor-house, Spinning-shop, and Seven Cottages the whole standing upon one acre of Land including a Garden and Yard'. (The poorhouse was sold to John Bushell, and converted by him into a brewery, and resold in 1840 to William Gardner of Bekesbourne.) In March 1837 it decided that £110 4s. 3d., the proceeds of sale of fixtures at the

34   The disused parish workhouse was bought, and converted into a brewery, by John Bushell in 1837. He sold it to William Gardner in 1840. White Post Brewery, to the west, with its maltings and the *First & Last*, was added in 1878. Seen here *c*.1875.

workhouse and the balance of the proceeds from the giving up of the School Farm tenancy, should be applied towards repayment of the loan due to the executors of Charles Horne; and next month resolved 'as ordered by the Board of Guardians' to write to the Poor Law Commissioners for consent to pay £591 2s. 3d.,

> the proceeds of sale of our Workhouse, now in the hands of the Treasurer of the Eastry Union, to Charles Horne's executors. We cannot reply to your request and furnish you with the Act of Parliament under which the cash was borrowed—but it was borrowed by the Parish and entered in the minutes of Vestry—We are all satisfied that the sum is due, and are most anxious to repay the same without delay.

Unrest on the part of the labourers continued right up until the new law came into force. In July 1835, the *Kentish Gazette* reported that 12 sheep, four ewes and eight lambs, had been found with their throats cut in a field at Ash belonging to Mr. Tomlin 'A patch of about twenty perches of unripe canary seed has also been cut down at night in that parish. The labourers and paupers are said to be in a very dissatisfied state in that neighbourhood.'

Nor did the new regime always turn out to be more benevolent than the old. When the local Guardians proposed to include in the weekly diet in the Eastry workhouse 'a pint of strong nourishing beef soup mixed with rice and vegetables', the assistant Poor Law Commissioner responsible for the Kent Unions was horrified, 'It would instantly make your poor house attractive, and break the spirit of your independent labourer … No country in the world can afford to feed its paupers on such a diet.'

ELEVEN

TRAVEL THROUGH ASH

The road between Ash and Sandwich has followed at least six successive routes. After the Romans left Britain, their steep straight road over Mount Ephraim was deserted in favour of a gentler, more circuitous route. Turning south-east just beyond Ash church down Moat Lane, it wound round the base of Mount Ephraim (where it is deeply sunken, often a sign of age and former importance), and so to Coombe. By the end of the 13th century this shadowed lane was known, doubtless for good reason, as Lovekys Street. For several centuries the road led north-east from Coombe, either through Marshborough or direct to Woodnesborough, on its way to Sandwich. At first the causeway across the marshes from Sandwich evidently reached only as far west as the leper colony at the 'Mauldry', north-west of the present roundabout. (Between the Mauldry and Sandwich the causeway must be earlier than the drainage dykes because it does not cut through them; further west, where it does, it must be later than the dykes.) Later, with the completion of the western end of the causeway soon after 1290, the route to Sandwich from Coombe no longer needed to turn south-east to Marshborough. Instead, it led north-eastwards, through Each to the causeway. But it was still a very winding route by Lovekys Street, and it was probably not long before the 'New Street' was laid out between Ash and the turn to Each at Houndpits. New Street formed part of the main route between Ash and Sandwich until well into the 18th century, almost certainly until after Peter Fector, a Dover banker, bought the manors of Levericks and Hills Church Gate in 1760, and Street End House was built, probably to replace Hills Court. By this time Sandwich had long since sunk into insignificance, but ships of the Royal Navy were almost always at anchor in the Downs, Deal was thriving, and the road through Ash was an important one.

Each parish had to keep up its own roads. In 1711 the Ash Vestry ordered that

> A rate be Made for & Toward ye Mending ye highways As followeth Viz: That Every Person that Occupyeth Ten Pounds p. Year Shall be Obliged to go One Day in every Year with a Court to ye Highways, And he that Useth Twenty Pounds p. Year one Day with Hutch or two days with a Court and so in Proportion for every Greater Quantity.

Gravel and shingle were carted to repair the roads, and snow was cleared. In 1768 the parish officers paid 'for Bear the labourers had when Mending Lay Lane and other places packing Trades [treads, i.e., ruts] 4s. 6d.'

73

Travel by road was expensive, and slow. In May 1758 it was announced that the Deal stage coach would set out from Deal to Canterbury at 1 p.m. on Tuesdays and Thursdays, and return from Canterbury at 9 a.m. on Wednesdays and Fridays. Passengers from Canterbury were asked to be punctual so that the coach could reach Deal by 1 p.m. It expected, therefore, to take four hours to cover the 18-mile journey. 'Passengers and parcels to London or any part of the road' would be taken in 'as usual'.

Sailing vessels ran from London along the north Kent coast: in 1677 the church-wardens had 'pd for one bible fourtyfive shillings and the hoyman for bringing them down from London on shilling'.

By 1798, but perhaps not long before, to cut off the long detour by New Street through Houndpits and Each, an entirely new coach-road was built across the fields to link Ash with the western end of the causeway. This new road cut across the old lanes— Cherry Garden and Hills Court Lanes, and Saunders and Goss Hall Lanes—and passed very close to Street End House. Perhaps, after buying Goss Hall in 1781, Fector had already moved away. But even so, the Deal road through Ash was still described in 1799 as 'the worst out of Canterbury'. At last, in 1802, 'An Act for repairing, altering, widening and improving the Road leading from the City of Canterbury to the Town and Port of Sandwich, in the County of Kent' (42 Geo.III Cap.6) was passed, a turnpike trust was formed, and toll-gates were set up: at St Martin's Hill in Canterbury and at the 'Street End' and the 'Each End' of the new length of road at Ash. Instead of using statute labour on the turnpike road, the Ash surveyors of the highways paid the trust an annual 'composition' of £12 3s. 9d.

TOLLS TO LET.
Turnpike Road from Canterbury to Sandwich.
NOTICE IS HEREBY GIVEN,

THAT a MEETING of the Trustees of the above Road, will be holden (by adjournment) at the "DOG INN," at WINGHAM,
On MONDAY, the 15th day of December next,
at 12 o'clock at Noon.
at which Meeting the TOLLS payable at the Three Turn-pikes, at or near St. Martin's Hill, Ash Street, and Each End, upon the said Road,
WILL BE LET BY PUBLIC AUCTION,
To the highest bidder, for the term of THREE YEARS, to be computed from the hour of 12 at night of the 31st DECEMBER next, in the manner directed by the Acts of Parliament passed for regulating Turnpike Roads in England, which Tolls produced during the last year the several sums following, viz. :—

	£	s.	d.
ST. MARTIN'S HILL GATE	493	1	0
ASH STREET and EACH END GATES	255	5	0

and will severally be put up at such sums.
Whoever happens to be the highest bidder will be required to pay down a deposit of £75, and at the same time to name one or two sufficient surety or sureties to the satisfaction of the said Trustees for the due payment of the rent quarterly in advance and for the performance of the covenants in the lease.
WIGHTWICK and KINGSFORD,
Clerks.
Canterbury, 10th November, 1862.

35   The Canterbury and Sandwich Turnpike. The right to collect the tolls at Ash Street and Each End Gates was to be let to the highest bidder (from an advertisement in the *Kent Herald*, 13 November 1862).

The first regular official post 'unto the City of Canterbury, Sandwich, Deal and the Downs', established in 1662, was by post-horse. From 1697 Wingham was a post-town, one of the smallest in Kent.

In March 1799, Thomas Austin was convicted of robbing the mail on the road between Sandwich and Canterbury, and executed. An immense crowd gathered on Charing Heath to see his body hanging in chains.

The first Dover mail-coach through Canterbury ran in 1785, but although permission to establish a Canterbury–Deal mail-coach was given in 1792, it did not run until March 1823. Even then, the Deal mail was drawn by only two horses, and had the reputation of being the slowest in the country. In October 1836, a Receiving-house for the post was established in Ash: the bag was made up at Wingham and forwarded by the Deal coach to the Ash Receiver, William Ralph, who delivered in the village.

36 The turnpike gate at Street End, *c.*1875. The turnpike trust came to an end about November 1876, and in 1877 Edward Goldup of *The Lion* bought the gatekeeper's cottage.

By 1836, besides the mail, four coaches made a daily return journey between Canterbury and Deal. One was licensed to carry four passengers inside and five outside; one to carry two inside and seven outside; one two inside and four outside; and one three inside and only one outside. Better though the macadam surfaces of the turnpike roads now were, in winter snow often stopped all travel by road, and Christmas 1836 was particularly bad. William Friend of Weddington kept a record:

1836 December 23: On this day the weather became colder, and on the next day, Saturday the 24th ... towards night the wind became very high, with a heavy fall of snow and hail, which on Sunday morning had drifted so as to make the road impassable ... The Mail coach with great difficulty reached Canterbury on Sunday morning, but the letter bags were forwarded from a little this side of Canterbury by a man on foot ... We have had no mail coach to this day (3rd Jan '7) reach Ash for several days; the mails have been forwarded by a horse from Canterbury. The Bye-roads are impassable; at present I cannot get a waggon or cart from Weddington ... On the sixth, the Mail reached Ash for the first time by coach. On Saturday, 7th, on my way to Canterbury I passed between two walls of snow, in some instances as high as the top of the carriage ... Many sheep have been dug out of the snow alive, after having been completely buried from 10 to 13 or 14 days, and have recovered and have done well.

37   Ash post office, *c.*1875. The Post, Money Order & Telegraph Office, Savings Bank and Government Annuity and Insurance Office had first opened in Ash in 1836. 'Letters arrive from London & all parts via Sandwich, and thence by mailcart at 5 a.m., delivered at 7 summer & 7.30 winter & 12.20 p.m.; box closes at 8.45, dispatch at 9 p.m.' Charles Brisley, the 'Receiver', was also a bootmaker and a photographer. Beyond was the sign of the *George & Dragon*, 'Cobb & Co.'s Margate Ales: Prop. James Prett'; opposite was the entrance to a blacksmith's forge.

The coming of the railways changed the scene. The South Eastern Railway's main line from London Bridge and Ashford through Canterbury to Ramsgate, with stations at Grove Ferry and Minster, opened on 13 April 1846, and its branch from Minster to Sandwich and Deal, passing through the parish, on 1 July 1847. The nearest station on the Canterbury to Dover section of the London, Chatham & Dover Railway, opened in 1861, was six miles away at Adisham. In 1864 Planché wrote

Ash Street, through which, not many years ago, the Deal mail dashed twice a day, and which well-laden stage-coaches from Walmer to Canterbury, Herne Bay and London, kept continually alive with the clatter of four horses and the echoes of the guard's horn, is now rarely traversed by anything more imposing than a neighbouring farmer's dog-cart, a parson's pony chaise, or mine host of the Lion's daily omnibus to Canterbury.

In fact, the tolls on the Ash Street and Each End gates, which had produced (clear of the gatekeepers' salaries) £245 17s. 11d. in 1832, still produced £255 5s. in 1861. But in 1877 the turnpikes were removed, the gatekeepers' cottages sold, and the trust dissolved. (The sharp fork at Street End and the two gatekeepers' cottages remain; so did the blind corner at Each End until the construction of the Ash by-pass in 1993.)

The railways took traffic from both roads and sea. By 1897 the Sandwich Hoy Company was operating only a weekly service to London, for goods. But carriers still plied daily between Canterbury and Sandwich, and in 1899 Alfred Howard had his own 'handsome and well-horsed' omnibus at 'The Lion Commercial Inn and Posting House', running three times daily to and from Sandwich with passengers and parcels. In the 1890s hopes were raised for increased traffic through Ash (and more trade) by a proposal for a new road-bridge below Paramour Street over the Stour to Thanet, only to be dashed by the decision to build it at Pluck's Gutter, in Stourmouth parish on the road north from Wingham without direct access to Ash.

In 1898 S. Pearson & Son, constructing the new Admiralty Harbour at Dover, laid out a light railway to Stonar gravel pit from the South Eastern & Chatham Railway's main line at Richborough Castle, crossing the river Stour by a swing-bridge, to carry the 5-6,000 tons of ballast they needed every week until about 1906.

THE GODFREYS OF BROOKE HOUSE

Thomas Jull, who lived at Goldstone on the estate inherited by his second wife Elizabeth Masters, died in 1799. Through his grandmother Amy Godfrey he was descended from Thomas Godfrey of Sellinge, who had had 20 children by two wives and several of whose sons had gone to London to seek their fortunes as merchants. One of them was Sir Edmund Berry Godfrey, the London justice who, having reported his examination of Titus Oates alleging a Popish Plot to the Privy Council on 28 September 1678, disappeared on 12 October, and whose dead body, strangled and transfixed with his own sword, was found on Primrose Hill on 17 October. Another was the father of Michael Godfrey, a founder and first deputy governor of the Bank of England in 1694, a great merchant and banker of celebrated integrity, who was killed by a cannon ball while talking to William III in the trenches before Namur in 1695.

They were rich men, but in two generations, for lack of male heirs, the family wealth passed down female lines. As was the fashion in such circumstances, they required the heiresses' husbands to adopt the family surname. So in 1799, by private Act of Parliament, Thomas's son, also Thomas Jull, of Brooke Street, assumed his great-grandmother's maiden surname of Godfrey. He became High Sheriff of Kent in 1802, and member of Parliament for Hythe from 1802 until his death in 1810, when his heir and nephew, John Jull (1789-1861), in turn adopted by Royal Licence the surname of Godfrey.

As a young man John Godfrey made a Grand Tour through the Mediterranean countries and the Near East, taking with him a young architect, Charles Barry, whose reputation was made by the drawings he brought back to England. Settled in Ash, John Godfrey turned to Barry to remodel Brooke House for him. Between 1835 and 1840, he transformed the exterior of the Elizabethan house, by facing it with stucco, adding buttresses and a Gothick battlemented porch and, his favourite feature, a Renaissance campanile. (Barry went on, of course, to design the new Houses of Parliament in the 1840s.)

John Godfrey, his sons Ingram Godfrey (1827-1916) and Colonel Albert Godfrey (1830-1924) (who as a younger son practised for many years as a solicitor in Queen Anne's Gate, SW in partnership with his uncle George Jull), and his grandson Hamilton Godfrey (1864-1930) lived at Brooke House in considerable style with a large household. They possessed a gallery of fine pictures, particularly Venetian view paintings by Francesco Guardi (collected in Venice by John Godfrey's father-in-law John Ingram, whose son Hughes Ingram left them to Ingram Godfrey). There was also a pair of portraits of John Godfrey and his wife Elizabeth by Sir Thomas Lawrence.

Some time in the 1920s Barry's rendering was removed from Brooke House (though his campanile remained), and it was returned to a half-timbered appearance. It was requisitioned in 1940, and the Godfreys never lived there again. It was demolished about 1951.

38 Ingram Godfrey's 13 female domestic staff (and a boy) at Brooke House, c.1910.

39 Brooke House, *c.*1910. About 1830 Charles Barry (1795-1860), commissioned by John Godfrey, had given the Tudor timbered manor house an 'Italian' make-over with campanile and water gardens.

40 Brooke House, again restored to the appearance of a Kentish manor house for Hamilton Godfrey about 1925, though the campanile and water gardens remained. It was demolished *c.*1950.

The Schools

At the dissolution of Wingham College in 1548, the royal commissioners reported that 'there hath not been any Gramer Schole kept'. In 1579, soon after John Stybbinge's arrival in Ash, the archbishop granted him a licence to teach in the parish, the first of a series lasting at least up to 1638, so there was then a school for boys, though probably not for girls. By 1629 John Proude had provided by will for his son to set up 'upon some part of his lands bounding upon Ash Churchyard a convenient house for the use of the parish for a School-house and store-house'. The churchwardens' complaint that the son 'hath set yp the frame of a house, but it is neither covered, walled or boarded' seems to have brought no result, so that the school was for many years held in a room above the church porch. In 1634 the churchwardens paid 3s. 10d. 'for mending of the glass windowes of the Church lofte or scolle houes', and 1s. 'to henary waties, scoole master, for writing of A Jaylle ses'. The master's salary and the other expenses depended upon better-off parishioners' subscriptions. The parish officers sold for 5s. the 'oulde clothes' of an 'oulde scholemaster' who had died, presumably receiving poor relief.

In 1720 Ash was one of 44 places in Kent (including Sandwich, Wingham and Staple) with a school. It then had 20 pupils, but in 1721 it was generously endowed, and opened to girls. Gervase Cartwright, a City merchant living at Guilton Rectory, died aged 44, a bachelor. His elder sisters, Eleanor and Anne, survived him less than a year, but in that time settled a farm at Guilton on trustees so that 25 boys and 25 girls might be taught 'in the charity school of Ash now maintained by the subscriptions of charitable persons for teaching poor boys to read and write and such other things as are suitable to their condition and capacity'. The Molland chancel in the church was long partitioned off as a schoolroom for the girls of the Cartwright School. When in 1819 further alterations were proposed, Elizabeth Godfrey gave property in The Street, where she had already converted an oast to serve as a schoolroom, to increase the number of children to 70, and to provide rent-free houses for the master and mistress, as well as two almshouses. In 1832, under her will, she left the trustees £1,000.

When Queen Victoria succeeded to the throne on 20 June 1837, it was Lord Conyngham who, as Lord Chamberlain and in company with Archbishop Howley, told her the news at Kensington Palace early that morning. (Conyngham's mother, the Dowager Marchioness, for many years the rapacious mistress of George IV and as plump as he was, owned Bifrons Park at Patrixbourne and, later, bought three farms in Ash parish.) At Ash, in February 1840, a dinner was given to the schoolchildren to celebrate 'the Queen's Nuptials' (and 'a ball took place at the *Ship Inn* which was very respectably attended'). Nearly three years later, William Friend wrote in his diary:

> 1842 November 10: The Queen and Prince Albert passed through this village on their way to Walmer Castle ... I had a good view of Her Majesty who with Prince Albert were in a large coach drawn by four wight horses from the 'Fountain'; the children were in a coach following. Her Majesty appeared very short, draped in a small silk bonnet; Albert was seen by my daughter sitting by the side of the Queen, dressed plain. She thought him very good looking, rather pale or sallow. He bowed to the people as he passed thro' the triumphal arches at the upper end of the street where were Cartwright's Charity children in line, the girls within the yard over the wall, the boys in line on the opposite side of the road ...

41 Queen Victoria and Prince Albert driving beneath the archway constructed outside the Cartwright School in Ash Street, on their way to Walmer, 10 November 1842, from the *Illustrated London News*.

More property was acquired in 1839 for a school playground, new schoolrooms for the boys were built in 1871, and a new girls' school about 1892.

In 1841 Thomas Kelsey of Fleet, whose own children had both died very young, built a separate infants' school on land in Chequer Lane given by Emmanuel College, to be run according to the rules of the 'Incorporated National Society for Promoting the Education of the Poor in the Principles of the Established Church'. At first supported by voluntary contributions and by the payment of 1d. per week for each child, it was endowed by Kelsey in 1860 with cottage property in Ash worth £68 a year, in order that no payment by the children would be necessary—a hope not fulfilled until 1891.

The Vestry resolved in 1870 that a separate school should be provided at Westmarsh, no doubt to forestall the possible building of a secular 'Board' school there under the Education Act 1870, and invited subscriptions towards the expected cost of £500. The new school and schoolhouse were up by 1873, at a cost of £583. The school closed about 1951.

At Ash, new buildings in their own playing field, to house the amalgamated Cartwright and Kelsey Schools, were opened in 1964, and later enlarged. Their design and materials proved to be so defective that by 1999 the governors, supported by the diocesan Education Committee, believed them beyond economic repair and asked that they should be demolished and rebuilt. However, the Kent Education Committee considered it was responsible for other schools in a worse state.

Independent education had been offered in the village as least as far back as 1870. Then, besides Mr. Richards' 'crammer's' establishment at the Vicarage, for young gentlemen intended for army or diplomatic careers, Miss Sarah Ann Marsh ran a 'preparatory school', and Miss Hannah Gorton a 'ladies' boarding school'. In 1878 Miss Marsh still had her 'preparatory school', and Miss Susan Becker Solley was running a 'ladies' school'. In 1899 and 1907 it was Mrs. Martha Marsh who had the 'ladies' school'. The schools' descriptions varied with the years: in 1878 Edwin Schenk had a 'commercial academy', in 1899 Edward Lombard Schenk a 'boys private school'; Harding Staines Schenk called it in 1924 a 'private business school', in 1930 a 'private school', and in 1934 a 'commercial school for boys and girls', in Chequer Lane.

In 1930 Ethel and Grace Elgar were running a school for small boys and girls in Poulton Lane, which they moved by 1934 to Reed Barn in Sandwich Road, but in 1940 had to evacuate to their own home at Crockshard Farm, Wingham. In 1956 Edna Cowell established a pre-preparatory school for under-11s at Guilton which she named Woottonley House School. She handed it over to Christopher Kirch in 1970, and retired. He turned the school into an educational trust but, after a period of very rapid expansion followed by almost equally quick decline, the school governors closed it in 1985. After a short gap, in 1987 Peter and Thelma Wrathall opened a new pre-preparatory school on the same site, calling it St Faith's, which prospered and was flourishing in 1999.

In 1990 the governors of Woottonley House set up two £40,000 funds at Kent College and St Edmund's School at Canterbury, to provide scholarships or grants at those schools, with preference given to boys or girls who had been to school in Ash or whose parents lived within five miles of Ash parish.

TWELVE

FARMING IN ASH 1600-1900

As early as 1582 many of the 350 Dutch settlers in Sandwich were market gardeners who had discovered the soil about the town to be 'exceedingly favourable to the growth of all esculent plants … The vegetables grew here in perfection, but much of them was conveyed … by water carriage to London'. Some came to live in Ash; in 1616 the churchwardens complained of 'Charles de Brooker a dutchman dwelling in our pishe who is negligent in coming to divine service having been sundry times admonished … but saith he frequenteth the dutch congregation in Sandwich'. Their skills benefited the local inhabitants 'whose tables were cheaply supplied with a variety of new and wholesome vegetables', and were also 'to the great advantage of the landholders, whose rents were considerably increased'. They also cultivated flax, canary and teazle, 'thus furnishing employment to the poor'.

42 Daniel Drayson of Weddington, market gardener and farmer, c.1875.

There were substantial farms in the parish in 1705: in 37 households there were 131 living-in farm workers and servants (or, in two cases, 'boarders'). Even so, 44 of those then described as 'day labourers' occupied at least some land. The parish rate assessments show that the number of small farms fell from about 1750, and again in the early part of the nineteenth century. John Boys remarked in 1796 on 'the putting together of small farms', and by 1841 the number of those in the parish who occupied land had almost halved since 1705, to less than one householder in five.

In 1779 Hasted described the Ash Level as 'very wet and unwholesome', but the southern part of the parish as 'very dry, pleasant and healthy', adding 'The soil in general is fertile, and lets on average at about one pound an acre; notwithstanding, there is a part of it about Ash-street and Guilton town where it is deep sand.'

To the roll-call of Ash volunteers in 1798 was appended an inventory of 'Cattle and Provision that may be removed from the parish' should the expected French invasion take place. It listed 206 oxen, 193 cows, 149 young cattle, 2,041 sheep, and 442 pigs; 1,295 quarters of wheat, 2,005 quarters of barley, and 260 quarters of oats; 387 loads of hay and 31 loads of straw; 27 sacks of potatoes and 10 sacks of flour, but 'beans and peas; none'; 196 draught horses and 27 riding horses; 48 (four-wheel) waggons and 83 (two-wheel) carts. The parish was clearly prosperous.

William Friend of Weddington kept a farm diary. In 1813 he sold a Margate butcher named Foat six heifers at £18 each, 10 'runts' at £22 each, and 48 wethers at 68s. each. In the same year Thomas Woodruff bought from him 41 sheep at Goldstone at 65s. and 56 sheep at Richborough at 63s. each, and in 1815, 10 'calve' (in-calf) heifers at £16 each. In 1813 his barley made 38s. a quarter, and oats 40s. In 1817 he 'carried 10 qrs Canary to Beal's hoy from oast'. In 1813 he hired two rams from Giles Grist of Brookland on Romney Marsh, one for 20 guineas, the other a yearling for 10 guineas, arranging 'to meet him with the rams on Saturday, the 30 [October], at half past 9 o'clock in the morning, at the Drum at Stanford'; their service performed, he returned them to Grist on 21 December.

43   Haymaking at Goss Hall, *c.*1905.

'In the vicinity of Sandwich there are a great many orchards which some years produce large quantities of excellent apples', John Boys wrote in 1796, 'most of which are sent by the coal vessels to Sunderland and Newcastle'. In 1813 Friend 'sold to John Elvery the apples and pears at Molland—reserving for myself all the Golden Pippins and Nonpariels, one sack of pudding apples, one bushel and a half of Corelip pears, and a large hand basket of Burgamer pears—for £80'.

Hops grown here, Boys wrote, were 'much sought after by the London brewers'. In 1813 Friend sold his hops at prices between £9 and £10 10s. a hundredweight to brewers at Sandwich, Deal and Canterbury.

At Michaelmas 1815 Friend noted that he had 'bargained with John Brenchley for waggoner's mate at Goldstone for 10 guineas per annum', and 'with John Thomas for waggoner at Molland for £15; to give him 15 guineas if he stays the whole year; to have no holidays but Christmas'.

44 Filled hop-pockets, stencilled as required by law with the name and number of the grower and the county, outside the oast at Moat Farm, 1912.

In 1796 Boys declared, 'Many [estates] in the eastern part of this county have been sold within these few years for 40, and some for 50, years purchase, and upwards'. Times changed, and in 1828 Sir Edward Knatchbull of Mersham, one of the members of Parliament for the county, believed that 'all farmers in Kent are insolvent'. Yet marshes on the Ash Level changed hands at £85 an acre in the 1820s; in 1831, Friend bought just under 31½ acres of marshland there for £2,450, over £78 an acre, and in 1841 he paid £2,180 at auction for 22 acres more, just under £100 an acre. In 1842 he 'agreed with Mr Collard of Sandwich for draining tiles and soles; the tiles at 45s. & soles at 12s. per thousand, making 57s. per thousand'. (In 1936, in a later time of agricultural depression, George Christopher Solley, himself a farmer, felt it necessary to explain, 'The entry refers to a practice then for a short time in vogue of draining land: the tiles and soles were made at Richborough Wall'.)

In the parish in 1840 there were 3,205 acres of arable, 3,146 acres of pasture or marsh, 116 acres of hop-gardens, 367 acres taken up by homesteads, gardens and orchards, and 36 acres of woodland. Partly because of the great size of the parish, it was always divided between many landowners. 'There is no great proprietor', Gleig wrote in 1832, even though Goshall with Levericks and the manor of Hills Church Gate,

Guston and Wingham Barton were all then owned by John Minet Fector of Kearsney Abbey, a banker in London and Dover. More surprisingly, for John Godfrey was to become a Deputy Lieutenant of Kent and his father had been High Sheriff, Gleig added, 'There is no resident gentleman in the parish', but perhaps the Godfreys then spent much time elsewhere. In the 1840s, the Dowager Marchioness Conyngham of Bifrons Park bought Goshall, Guston and Fleet.

Bagshaw's Directory of 1848 listed 49 farmers in the parish, of whom 10 were 'market gardeners'. Farmers still prospered, but had their problems: 1836 was a particularly difficult year. On 29 November occurred the 'November Gale', 'One of the greatest storms of wind I ever remember', Friend noted in his diary. 'Great injury has been done to all the neighbourhood; three barns in this parish levelled with the ground, and every house in the village has suffered more or less in the destruction of the tiling. Wheat stacks uncovered and, in some instances, half the roof blown off.' Only a month later, after the great snowfall at Christmas 1836, he wrote

> The wind and snow had rendered it impossible for the graziers to send men into the marshes to look after the sheep. My bailiff made the attempt, but was compelled to return. The next day he took with him several men; when they reached the marshes they found 8 dead, completely covered with snow in the ditches. The only way to discover them was with a long pole, to try the ditches. The following day, three more were driven into the ditch and died. Having only 103 sheep in the marshes, my loss has not been so great as many others. On Friday got the remaining 92 to Weddington on turnips.
>
> The loss of sheep has been greater than I ever remember: Mr. Wm Friend [his son] lost 73, Mr Culmer 76, Delmar 40, Mr Emmerson a great many. Indeed it is impossible to say at present what loss has been sustained. At present (the 31st Decr) we have had no account from Romney Marsh or any other parts; we have been completely isolated.

On 7 January he noted, 'The estimated loss of sheep on Romney Marsh was upwards [of] 10,000.'

In September 1844, the *Kentish Gazette* reported one of the worst storms for many years.

> The lightning was truly awful, the Heavens appearing with each flash a flame of liquid fire. Considerable damage has been done in the hop grounds. About ten o'clock a large barn, containing the whole produce of the farm (Guston), in the parish of Ash, belonging to Mr. Coleman, of Goss Hall, was discovered to be on fire. The destructive element spread with great rapidity to an adjoining barn stored with beans and barley, besides a bean stack, and ultimately consumed several outbuildings with some livestock, consisting of a fine bull, fifteen pigs, and one calf. The fire originated by the barn containing the wheat being struck with the electric fluid. The Kent engine, followed by the Phoenix from Canterbury, arrived at the scene of destruction soon after the alarm was given, but although every exertion was used to save the property, it is feared the damage will exceed £2000. The buildings are insured in the Sun, and the stock in the Norwich Fire Office.

Less than four years later, on 18 July 1848, the *Kentish Gazette* reported that, about three o'clock the previous Saturday morning, a barn at East Street occupied by Mr. Coleman had been struck by lightning and set alight.

The fire was so sudden and fierce from the dryness of the thatch that it was, with the wagon lodge and a straw stack, consumed before anything could be got out, and was all down before the engine from Sandwich got to the spot. There was a large quantity of wheat on the floor of the barn which had been thrashed on Thursday and Friday, about twenty quarters, part of which was not much damaged. The buildings and also the stock was insured.

In August 1846 John Godfrey's greenhouse at Brooke Street, 'severely injured by the hail storm of Saturday afternoon', had also been insured, in the Farmers' Hail Storm Insurance Office.

The labourers had come to accept that threshing by flail was disappearing. By 1865 John Ralph of Ash hired out threshing machines, working not only in the parish but also in the surrounding area, charging £1 10s. a day for a four-horse machine and £1 15s. for one with six horses. In 1867 he was using a steam engine, and charging 3s. an hour or, on piece-work, at the rate of (usually) 2s. 3d. a quarter for wheat or barley and 1s. 9d. for oats. He employed Thomas and William Hougham to feed the machine; in 1867 for eight weeks at £1, eight weeks at 18s., and eight weeks at 16s.; and in 1868 and 1869 for 12 weeks at £1, and 12 weeks at 18s. (The average farm wage in Kent went up from 11s. 9d. in 1824 to 16s. 6d. in 1872, but fell back to 14s. 6d. by 1892.)

Potato blight, believed to have been introduced from the United States, first occurred in east Kent in the autumn of 1844. Early in August 1845 a Mr. Parker, a large potato grower and wholesaler, reported in answer to a Home Office enquiry that he had driven round Ash, Sandwich and Wingham, and found the whole crop, early and late, and including potatoes in cottage gardens, entirely destroyed. (By September the blight had spread to Ireland, where about a million and a half people died in the resulting famine, and from where nearly another million emigrated in the next five years.)

Nevertheless, in 1864 Planché wrote that the value of pasture and arable land at Ash

> has nearly trebled during the present century, while its numerous and prolific gardens supply not merely the markets of all the neighbouring towns and watering-places; but to a very great extent even the celebrated one of Covent Garden, London, with fruit and vegetables; Mr. Thomas Sutton, of Ash, being one of the most considerable market gardeners in England.

John Ralph occasionally sold soft fruit. In July 1867, he charged 9d. for a gallon of gooseberries, 9d. for 6 lb. of redcurrants, and 2s. for 12 lb. of blackcurrants.

After 1870 farming incomes suffered from imported wheat from North America, and chilled meat from New Zealand. There was a renewed movement to split larger farms into smaller market-garden units. Sarah Whyman had inherited Knell Farm (250 acres) and Paramour Grange (233 acres) from her father Leonard Wheatley of Marylebone in 1854; in 1893 Knell was put up for sale in fifteen lots. In 1899 Moat Farm, then 170 acres in extent, was sold for £5,800, £34 an acre. In 1902 mortgagees foreclosed on Bird Thomas Stiff at Nash, the third generation of his family to farm a substantial acreage there and at Shatterling. Kelly's Directory listed 35 market gardens in the parish in 1899 (and 45 in 1924). In 1899 Charles Herbert farmed 130 acres at Twitham Hills, but kept poultry, producing 28,000 eggs a year, and grew apples, pears and cherries, and

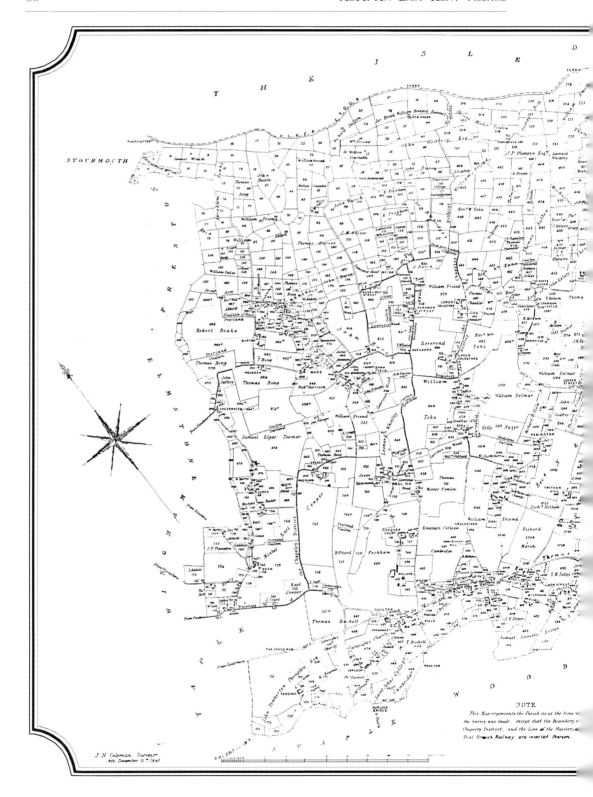

J N Coleman Surveyor.
Ash December 31st 1841

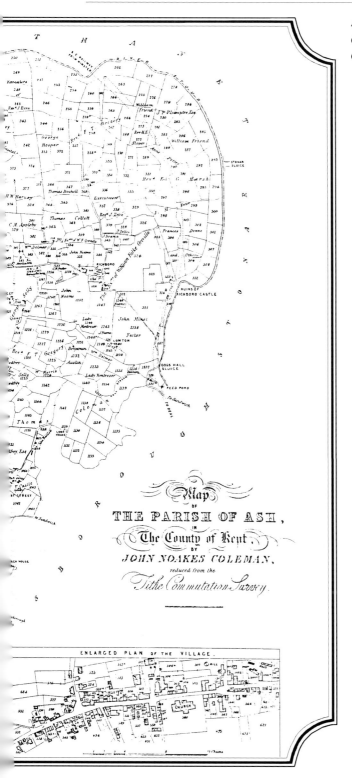

45   The parish of Ash reduced from the Tithe Commutation Survey of 1840, by J.N. Coleman, 1846.

46   A 'self-delivery' reaper, *c.*1910. Its revolving sails brought the corn to the knives, and threw it to one side, leaving the horse-walk clear for the next cut; the sheaves still had to be bound by hand.

47   This traction engine, seen outside its shed at Guilton *c.*1910, belonged to Mrs. Emma Ralph, 'threshing-machine proprietor'. It supplied steam-power for hauling and sawing as well as threshing.

48 Thomas Buddle's smithy at Cop Street, *c.*1895.

49 Milkers at Moat Farm, 1912.

50   The staff of Messrs. W.O. Chandler & Son, fruit-growers at Goldstone, *c.*1895.

strawberries, currants, gooseberries and raspberries, largely for the London market. At
Knell and New Street Henry Holness grew hothouse grapes for Covent Garden, as well
as asparagus. Percy Chandler grew both top fruit and soft fruit at Knell, and his brother
W.G. Chandler had about 40 acres of fruit at Goldstone, specialising in strawberries for
Covent Garden. Fred Court of Downfield sent fruit to wholesale markets in London,
Edinburgh, Glasgow and Aberdeen and to other northern towns, as well as sending a van
every other day to Ramsgate. Strawberries were packed in boxes or baskets at the farms,
and sent by waggon or rail to the markets. 'Now that better facilities and rates have been
granted by the railway companies,' it was said,

> growers have more inducement to increase their out-turn. In strawberries alone, the quantities
> despatched from Ash alone amount to many tons, while of other soft and quickly perishable
> fruits the supply for a time at least appears almost endless. Apples and pears are, of course, capable
> of storage until they are ready for the market and the market is ready for them ...

Day's Early Sunrise Pea, 'long since become a standard variety quoted in every
seed-merchant's catalogue', was first introduced by Henry Cook of Guilton, who claimed
the profits from it had paid for his new house at Cop Street, which he called 'Sunrise
Cottage'. At Weddington Charles Woodruff was a cattle salesman and auctioneer, a
business established by his grandfather in the 1850s or earlier, and F.W. & C. Petley had
been auctioneers and valuers for some twenty years at Guilton.

THIRTEEN

THE VICTORIAN VILLAGE

After 1831 the population of the parish fell: to 2,077 in 1841; 2,096 in 1851; and 2,039 in 1861 (obviously affected by the diphtheria epidemic). It rose slightly to 2,106 in 1871, to 2,198 in 1881, and 2,242 in 1891, but then began to fall again. In 1841 the average size of the 406 households in Ash was 5; but there were 62 of between 8 and 10 people, nine of between 1 and 13, four of 14 and one of 16. Emigration to the colonies evidently continued: in 1848 Thomas Reynolds, formerly of Goldstone Farm, died in Toronto aged 24, and in 1855 Lawrence Holttum, late of Weddington, died in Australia at the age of 36.

The countryside could be dangerous, even before the introduction of machinery. At Ash, in May 1831, John Spratt, aged about seven,

> was riding in a cart and had laid himself down in it, the driver having forgotten he was there; at the instant of backing the cart into the lodge where it usually stood, the little fellow jumped up, and his head coming in contact with a beam in the lodge, was crushed between that and the front of the cart and killed instantly.

In October 1853 George Baldock, an employee at Ash brewery, was driving a horse and cart near Elmstone on his way back to the brewery. 'The night being exceedingly dark, it is supposed the cart was driven on the bank at the side of the road, by which it was upset, and falling on Baldock, produced instant death'. In January 1856 a boy named Claringbould was killed by a threshing machine, and his grandmother 'was so much afflicted by the appearance of his mangled remains that she died in the course of the ensuing night'. In June 1857 a six-year-old boy, Shadrach Church, was in a meadow with his father seeing some sheep washed.

> His father having desired him to go home, he left for that purpose, as his father supposed, but who afterwards learnt that his son's cap had been picked up in the sheepwash, where it was seen by another son; on which a rake was obtained, and the boy drawn out quite dead.

In September 1855 John Ralph, aged nine, was also involved in an accident with a threshing machine, and seriously injured his foot; he was promptly taken to the Kent and Canterbury Hospital. Not all accidents were so serious; in May 1850, 13-year-old Benjamin Goodban of Ash fell out of a tree while birds' nesting, and broke his leg. 'He was immediately conveyed to the Kent & Canterbury Hospital, and is going on favourably.'

In June 1857, not far from Ash village, James Read was knocked down by a horse and cart 'which passed over him, and occasioned a fracture of the right thigh bone, a severe scalp wound, and contusions of the left arm. He was conveyed to the Kent and Canterbury Hospital where the necessary attentions were rendered, and he is progressing favourably.' In July 1855, the *Kentish Gazette* reported with grim humour what it described as a 'Curious Incident': 'The neighbourhood of Staple and Ash was recently visited by a mad-dog and several dogs were bitten by the rabid animal. One of the latter before being destroyed attacked a cat, and grimalkin bit a duck; and duck, cat and dog were forthwith destroyed.'

Among the catalogue of mostly minor crime in early Victorian Ash, usually resulting in short terms of imprisonment, and sometimes whipping, four men were sentenced to be transported (a punishment abolished in 1868), all for theft: in April 1838, William Sayer, for seven years, for stealing five pigs worth £3; in April 1841, Charles Port, for 10 years, for stealing a silver watch; in October 1846 Edward Sandwell, for 10 years, for stealing a piece of Scotch plaid waistcoat cloth (but nine months earlier, in January 1846, he had been sentenced to consecutive terms of two months' and four months' imprisonment for other thefts), and in 1850, Martin Trevor, 28, for 10 years, for stealing a watchguard, two silver thimbles and other articles. Some sentences seem harsh: in October 1837 James Ledner was committed to St Augustine's Gaol at Canterbury and, a fortnight later, sentenced to 14 days in the house of correction, for stealing four apples, valued at one penny, from William Doorne of Brooke Street; in February 1846 Richard Hardeman was sentenced at Kent Assizes to a month in the house of correction with hard labour, for the theft of a loaf of bread; and in June 1857, at Wingham Petty Sessions, George Solly pleaded guilty to stealing two small glasses, value 5d., from Edward Goulden of the *Chequer Arms*, and was sentenced to a month's imprisonment. But courts could be comparatively lenient, too: at Kent Assizes in April 1850, where Robert Elcome and Edward Pratt were convicted of stealing a sack of oats—'another case of stealing corn for their master's horses'—they were sentenced to just 10 days' imprisonment; and at East Kent Quarter Sessions in January 1857 when Thomas Hammond pleaded guilty to the theft of a sheaf of barley 'which, it appeared, he had taken for his master's horses', he was given 14 days' hard labour. Indeed, a court could disapprove of the prosecutor's own conduct: at East Kent Quarter Sessions in January 1850, Stephen Pilcher was charged with stealing fustian cloth from his master Robert Bubb. 'The chairman in summing up to the jury alluded to the too prevalent practice of masters not giving their servants an opportunity of attending divine worship on the Sabbath, and remarked some points in the case that had not been clearly marked out. Verdict, not guilty.'

Occasionally a court made it clear that it thought a case should not have been brought. In January 1860 the *Kentish Gazette* reported the prosecution before the Wingham magistrates of James Cook, a farmer, for assault on John Bourn, landlord of the *Marquis of Granby* at Ash. Bourn gave evidence that about half past nine on the evening of 17 December 1859 Cook had come into his house

much the worse for liquor. He wanted to have a pint of ale, which witness refused to supply him with. He then wanted to go into the back parlour, but witness would not allow him to do so, and sent for a policeman. As soon as the defendant heard the order given to fetch a policeman he became exceedingly violent, and complainant put him out of the house, but in doing so he did not use more force than was necessary. Immediately afterwards the defendant came back into the house, and struck him on the head, with the butt-end of his gun, saying at the same time that he would knock complainant's brains out.

Bourn said the blow severely bruised his neck, and cut his head. Cook did not appear before the Court. The magistrates convicted—but only fined Cook £3, and expenses.

At Michaelmas 1842 William Friend of Weddington 'agreed with Thomas Stokes as coachman, and indoors servant when required, at 18s. per week; to board himself, and to have the adjoining house should he marry or require it, but to take no inmates except a housekeeper'. He was to get a good bit more than the average farm wage.

In November 1854 George Ridout, the curate, called a meeting in aid of the Patriotic Fund, set up by *The Times* to supply comforts to the sick and wounded troops at Scutari in the Crimea, where Florence Nightingale had just agreed to go; £25 was subscribed at the meeting, and another £48 was collected in the village. 'The feelings of the poor are clear from the fact that out of 530 contributors, 200 gave sums varying from a penny to sixpence.' The following month news arrived of the death on 27 November, from cholera in the camp before Sebastopol, of Arthur Godfrey, the 25-year-old second son of John Godfrey of Brooke House, while serving as senior Lieutenant of the 1st Battalion, The Rifle Brigade, and already a veteran of campaigns in Canada and South Africa.

An epidemic, worse than anything previously known in Ash, broke out in November 1856. On 2 July a little girl aged 4 had landed at Folkestone from the Boulogne packet, seriously ill. She died next day, and two more deaths occurred in Folkestone that month from 'Boulogne sore throat'. The next case was at Ash, on 7 November. It was the first of many, only too often very rapidly fatal. Frequently children, well in the afternoon, were dead next morning. In one cottage, a family of seven children fell ill, and four died. In May 1857 the *Kentish Gazette* reported

> The disease of an apparently novel description which has proved so fatal to young children in this vicinity still continues with unabated vigour … Some parents have by it been deprived of the whole of their offspring. It is said so peculiar is the progress of the disease that it baffles the art of the medical profession.

By 10 November 1857, almost exactly a year after the first case, there had been about 300, 58 of them fatal, in Ash. Soon doctors came to call the new disease 'diphtheria'. The outbreak at Ash was not quite its first appearance, but it was this virulent epidemic which spread through east Kent and the whole country.

In January 1860 there was apprehension about what appeared to be aggressive intentions on the part of the French, England's traditional enemy. At a meeting held at the *Red Lion Inn* to form an Ash rifle corps, 73 members were enrolled and Captain Frederick Godden, late of the 56th Regiment and West Kent Militia, and part-owner of the Ash brewery, was chosen Captain, in what became the 24th Kent (Ash) Rifle Volunteers.

The Vestry resolved in 1849 that 'the Bell should be rung all the year round at 5 o'clock in the morning and at 8 o'clock in the evening during the winter'. But not all labourers now worked in the fields, away from a clock; the brewery was becoming the largest single employer. In December 1860 the *Kentish Gazette* reported that 'great improvements are in progress in the fine old village of Ash which is fast becoming more like a town with its genteel villas, good modern houses, and many newly erected respectable cottages built by the enterprising builder, Mr. R.R. Smith'.

Richard Ratcliff Smith had since 1849 built Prospect Place and Flint House south of New Street, and went on to build Lavender Place in New Street, Greenhill Place in Sandwich Road, and Victoria Terrace, Alexandra Row, and Havelock Place in The Street, all for rent, before his death in 1872.

In 1864 Planché admitted that only 'a few gingerbread stalls and "knock-em downs" continue to do duty for the "fair"'. But if the twice-yearly village fairs on 5 April (Old Lady Day) and 11 October (Old Michaelmas) had almost gone, he loyally (as the curate's father-in-law) praised Ash's good fellowship, 'its gay cricket matches, its joyous school feasts, its merry May games, and its genial harvest homes. For the celebration of these two last—time-honoured and truly English festivals—it has lately indeed acquired a high and well-merited county reputation.'

He might have added more: concerts, dramatic performances, a catch club, a 'Tonic Solfa' singing class, cricket matches, and even two small race-meetings in 1858 at Molland. In June 1849 the *Canterbury Journal* advertised 'a foot-race for £10 a side, distance 100 yds, between Charles Reynard of Ash and Henry Setterfield of Monkton— next Monday at Ash'.

In 1848 Ash village was still described as 'large and considerable'. There were five inns and a beer-house; four grocers, two butchers, a pork butcher and a baker; a chemist; four boot-and-shoe makers, three tailors, drapers and hatters, and a straw-hat maker; a hairdresser; a cabinet-maker; two plumbers, a carpenter, builder and wheel-wright, a stonemason, and a bricklayer and plasterer; three corn-millers; two black-smiths, two saddlers and harness-makers, and a (horse) collar-maker; as well as a brewer, a surveyor, two surgeons, a veterinary surgeon, and a farrier. There was also an inn, a carpenter, builder and wheelwright, a boot-and-shoe maker, and a shop at Westmarsh; a beer-house, a blacksmith, and a shop at Ware; a beer-house at Nash; and a blacksmith at Cop Street.

In 1867 'S. Solly, Grocer Baker & Provision Merchant', next to the *Ship*, advertised himself as established in 1812; Bourne's butchery opposite had been in business there since about 1806; Charles Harden's draper's shop, established in 1844, with a yearly turnover by 1853 of up to £6,000, and book debts of £2,000, served customers as far away as Dover; and in 1857 Israel Jacobs had set up his East Kent Stores facing the village pond at the bottom of Chequer Lane. By the turn of the century Harden's had as many as 10 milliners working on its top floor. For some years a second brewery, White Post Brewery, adjoining the *First and Last* in Sandwich Road and very close to Gardner's brewery, was in operation, but it failed, and in August 1878 its stock-in-trade was sold by auction. Besides the brewing utensils and 500 various beer-casks, there were

> a strong well-built covered wagon to carry 4 tons, with double shafts; an excellent 4-wheel dray to carry 50 cwt, with double and single shafts; a 4-wheel wagon; a 2-wheel cart on springs; a light spring cart; a dog-cart with cushions and lamps complete; and a four-wheel phaeton with cushion, etc. complete.

51   Messrs. Jacobs Brothers' shop was established in 1857: 'Grocers, Tea, Foreign & British Wine
Dealers, Wine & Spirit Merchants, & Birmingham, Sheffield and Staffordshire General Warehousemen'.
For the benefit of the photographer, William Morris, the Ash 'high constable', had come out of his
barber's shop next door, and so had William Stiff from his baker's shop opposite.

52   The Street, *c*.1890. Charles Watson, Grocer and Tea Dealer, had taken over John Grout's shop by
1878. The three policemen were still intrigued by the photographer's apparatus. (From another set of
photographs of about 1890, most of which are probably also by Boyer.)

53   George Cornwell, delivering groceries for Charles Watson, *c.*1890.

54   Stephen Solley described himself as a grocer and baker, 'established 1812', but also displayed hardware in his window, *c.*1875.

55 Henry Harrison (1860-1925), who worked in The Street as a butcher for Henry Bourne, seen here in the uniform of the 24th Kent (Ash) Rifle Volunteers, *c*.1878.

56 Victoria Terrace, *c*.1900. The shop belonged to John Swinnock, originally a tailor, and Alfred Beer, originally a tailor and baker, but now 'Tobacconists and Fancy Dealers; fancy and view china, vases, toys and games; Waterbury watches 10/6d.' Already, 'Anybody committing a nuisance in this alley will be prosecuted'. The terrace, built in the 1860s and named after the widowed Queen, was followed by Alexandra Row (after Alexandra of Denmark, married to the Prince of Wales in 1863), and Havelock Place (after Sir Henry Havelock, a hero of the India Mutiny of 1857), 23 cottages in all, built with others in Ash by Richard Ratcliff Smith, who died in 1872. Earlier, Lydia Sample and Ann Kennard both worked as dressmakers from cottages in Victoria Terrace. At the far end, Walter Measday's pork-butchery had (like Henry Bourne's butcher's shop) a canopy to keep off the sun.

The brewery itself was put up for sale by auction in September 1878 at the *Bell Hotel*, Sandwich, and was bought, with the *First and Last*, by Austen Gardner of Gardner's brewery, for £1,000.

One of the more colourful village businesses was William Dixon's chemist's shop, established by his father Frederick in the 1840s. In 1899, besides the pharmacy proper, it was a newsagent's and tobacconist's, included a lending library, and stocked 'many pretty and fashionable nick-nacks suitable for presents'. Among the shop's specialities, on sale since the 1860s, was 'Dixon's Antholeon', advertised as

> a cure for burns, wounds, bruises, chilblains, and all abrasions or external injuries to the skin, and the treatment of erysipelas, rheumatic gout, piles, etc., very rapidly reducing inflammatory symptoms and reducing pain. Antholeon, too is extensively used in the nursery, and is also useful in the case of horses and domestic animals.

57   The *Chequers Inn* (Rigden's Faversham Brewery: Prop. Charles Clayson), *c*.1875. The *Chequers*, the *Lion* and the *Ship* were three of the original inns of the village.

58 The *Lion*, 'Commercial Inn and Posting House: Gardner's Ash Brewery: Prop Edward Goldup', *c*.1875. 'Goldup's Omnibus' left the *George & Dragon* and *Saracen's Head*, Canterbury, for Ash every day at 4 p.m. Goldup was also the Collector of Taxes. Edward Wells, collarmaker, had a horse-collar over his shoulder; his thatched shop was opposite, next to that of James Fells, cabinet-maker.

59 The *Good Intent*, 'Gillow's East Kent Brewery, Sandwich: Prop. John Chapman', *c*.1875. It closed in 1919, with several other alehouses in The Street.

It had a wide local reputation, and was still available from Dixon's successors in business in Ash in the 1950s.

Dixon also acted as secretary of the Ash-next-Sandwich Gaslight, Coal and Coke Company. In 1865, following the Company's formation, the Vestry resolved to adopt the Lighting and Watching Act 1833 'for the district between Molland Lane and Cherry Garden Lane, and to raise not more than £35 for the purpose'. In 1872 it appointed, apparently for the only time, voluntary parish constables.

In 1838 the Vestry had noted that there were 30 miles of roads in the parish for which it was responsible. Asked in 1869 if the new highway board created under the Highway Act 1866 had given satisfaction to the ratepayers, it replied, 'The expenditure has increased nearly 20 per cent, and the roads are not any better; they were in a good state previously.' But in 1880 it agreed to transfer the entire management of the roads to the Eastry Board of Guardians. In 1894 all the Vestry's functions, except those relating to the church, as well as the churchwardens' civil powers, passed to the new Parish Council. At the first Parish Meeting, held in the Cartwright School on 4 December 1894, there were at least 135 electors present, and 27 candidates for membership of the Council. A poll was demanded and held, and the first meeting of the new Council took place on 31 December. Ingram Godfrey, who had not put up for election as a councillor, was elected its first chairman.

60 On Mount Ephraim, on a summer Sunday afternoon in the 1890s.

In 1889 the Local Government Board's medical officer sharply criticised the 'impure and ineffective water supplies' in Ash, where there had been no less than 40 recent outbreaks of typhoid. After an inquiry by the Board into drainage at Ash, the Eastry Board of Guardians in 1891 bought land south of Pudding Lane for sewage disposal works, but for several years much of the new Parish Council's time was taken up by complaints that these works were unable to deal with the effluent from Gardner's brewery. Although it could be said in 1899 that Ash was 'well supplied with good and pure water', there was still reason to criticise

> a system of drainage which the urban district authorities no doubt thought a veritable sanitary engineering success … We are sorry to say that, although the scheme may work well enough in one sense, the effluent, which is discharged into the Durlock stream, does not cause that 'purling brook' to smell quite so sweetly as the lily or the rose! … This tiny rivulet frowns—it was once a smiling stream—as it meanders through the sister parishes and whispers to them with perfumed (?) breath of the wonders of nineteenth century civilisation!

(Sadly, the system was still overloaded in 1999, so that after heavy rain, despite the efforts of generations of sanitary engineers, manholes burst open to discharge their awful contents before the front doors of houses in Pudding Lane, and thence into the same Durlock stream.)

FOURTEEN

VICTORIAN CHURCH AND CHAPEL

In 1829, Gleig told Quarter Sessions that there were in Ash 'three small places of worship regularly licensed, and the gross number of Dissenters amounts to 28 families containing about 90 souls. Of these 6 families belong to the Baptist persuasion, 12 to that of the Wesleyan Methodists, and 11 to the Independent Calvinists.' In his farewell sermon in 1834 he said

> In matters of religion there are very few parishes of equal extent with this where greater unanimity prevails. There are indeed among you some who worship God elsewhere than in the established church; but their numbers are altogether inconsiderable; whereas, the ordinary congregations which attend here present a spectacle which cannot fail to gladden the hearts of all who desire to preserve the unity of the spirit in the bond of peace.

In 1842, largely by the exertions of the curate, Francis Russell Nixon, before his consecration that year as first Bishop of Van Diemen's Land, Holy Trinity Church was built at Ware, and in 1849 Westmarsh became a separate ecclesiastical parish.

In 1850 the Church of England was beset by the rise of tractarianism within its ranks, and by secessions from it to the Catholic Church. When in September Pope Pius IX created the Catholic archbishopric of Westminster and twelve diocesan bishoprics, there was uproar. The *Kentish Gazette* reported on 26 November that, at Ash,

> in compliance with the wishes of the Perpetual Curate and Churchwardens of this parish (as expressed by a printed handbill extensively circulated among the parishioners) a meeting was held in the endowed School-room on Thursday evening, which was both numerously and respectably attended, the Rev. G. Ridout in the chair, to memorialise the Queen and the Archbishop of Canterbury on the recent papal aggression.

In the last five years (1843-8) of Edward Penny's ministry at Ash, recorded communicants at Easter averaged 200, and at Christmas 161. During the incumbencies of George Ridout and Henry Mackarness (1852-7 and 1863-8) the corresponding averages were 115 and 115, and 115 and 101. Yet in April 1859 Mackarness wrote

> It is much to be wished that more room could be provided in our overcrowded Parish Church. There is space enough, if only the unsightly and inconvenient square pews were removed ...; the sittings are but 630; at least 200 more might be gained by rearrangement, and it is to be hoped that our always liberal Parish will not refuse to do what is so much needed.

However, in June of that same year, 1859, James Barton Dadd, the Independent pastor, expressed a different view. He described how the old chapel, built in 1806 and seating about 100, had been found far too small 'owing to a want of evangelical doctrine in the establishment and an evident sympathy on the part of the Inhabitants with Congregational dissent', and had been replaced in 1849 by a new chapel which, with a lately added gallery, seated 300. It was, he said, a wonder that the congregation, until then without a resident pastor, had not fallen away, and he could 'only attribute our present position to a dearth of spirituality in the Established Church'.

In 1861 Dadd reported that the Independent chapel now had 88 members. They had by 1859 become so dissatisfied with the Sandwich chapel, of which Ash was part, that they had determined to sever the link with Sandwich and to appoint Dadd as pastor. There was bitterness on both sides, and the breach was not healed for eight years. Then, after the Ash members had confessed their error and 'the wrong done to the pastor and members of the church at Sandwich', the Ash chapel was reinstated—and thereafter tacitly allowed to go its own way. In 1869 it was enlarged again: it already had outposts at Barnsole and Goldstone. Dadd left Ash in 1871. In 1883 the Congregational Church, as it was by then known, built a Sunday School (cost £520), and in 1885 acquired from the Deal church an organ (£45), and in 1891 a silver Communion service (the gift of William Oldfield Chandler, whose son gave the individual cups which members resolved to adopt in 1912). But by 1893 church membership had risen only to 94. A Primitive Methodist chapel was built in 1871 at Cooper Street, and a Wesleyan chapel, replacing an earlier one, at Westmarsh in 1896.

Of the 11 successive perpetual curates at Ash between 1803 and 1869 the youngest was aged 25 on appointment, the oldest 47: their average age was 32. In general they were without private means, but they came from educated, socially assured backgrounds; they were energetic, and they expected (and were expected) to lead the parish. Henry Mackarness (1857-68) had been 12th man in the Eton cricket XI, and a scholar and Fellow of King's, Cambridge. In the Vicarage he boarded pupils, many of them Old Etonians, to prepare them for the army examinations. The boys strengthened the village cricket team for matches at Molland and, coached by his wife Matilda and her father, Planché, the historian of Ash who was a professional playwright and pantomime librettist, put on amateur theatricals, girls from the local Gardner and Bushell families supplying the female parts, and concerts. In 1862 Mackarness revived the village maypole festivities, and (not without opposition from village publicans who feared a loss of trade) a Harvest Home celebration for the whole parish. But he died at Ash, of erysipelas, in December 1868, aged only 41.

The appointment of his successor, John Richards, aged 55, in 1869 marked a watershed. He was the first of several incumbents—now 'vicars'—who had spent their earlier careers in the mission field: Richards himself (1869-84), 17 years in India; Francis Michell (1901-19), 30 years in China and India; Conrad Barton (1919-34), 11 years in Newfoundland; Charles Magraw (1934-45), three years in India; and Cyril Carter (1945-58), six years in the Persian Gulf. Of the twelve appointed since 1869, their average age on appointment was 46; only three were under 50, and two were 61. Unsurprisingly, many of them lacked the energy and drive of younger men. So in the established church, too, the numbers of Easter and Christmas communicants rose scarcely

61   St Nicholas Church, 1897, from a drawing by Phil May (1864-1903).

62   The chancel in St Nicholas Church, *c.*1890.

at all, to average 122 and 106 in 1878-93, despite the fact that Richards presented 366 candidates for confirmation in 11 years.

There were changes inside the church at Ash: the Molland chancel had been re-opened in 1835; a new pulpit and reading-desk under the tower-crossing were provided in 1854; and new Communion rails, given by Bishop Nixon, and a new stained-glass east window, designed by Thomas Willement, in 1856. In 1861 Emmanuel College restored the Molland chancel and, in the same year, the Eccle-siastical Commissioners undertook the restoration of the high chancel, under the supervision of Ewan Christian. Until the 1860s the churchwardens had maintained the church and provided for its services by means of church rates, payable by every ratepayer in the parish. In 1860 and 1862 there was opposition to the organist's salary (£10 p.a.) and refreshments for confirma-tion candidates being met from the church rate and, on the passing of the Compulsory Church Rates Abolition Act 1868, the churchwardens gave notice that they would not be personally responsible for the clerk's, organist's and sexton's salaries. In 1870, and for many years afterwards, a committee collected subscriptions in the parish. Collections were not then regularly taken at services, but in 1872 it was agreed that 'to meet the additional expenses incurred by the Sunday Evening service, a collection be made at the door every Sunday evening'. In August 1875 it was announced that

> The face of Ash Church Clock requires painting and the hands and figures gilding. The estimated cost of the work required is £13 10s. which includes scaffolding and all incidental expenses. As the church funds are not equal to this additional burden and as there are many who although not

subscribers to the church funds would probably be willing to contribute towards the repair of the parish clock, it has been thought desirable to raise a separate subscription for defraying the cost of the work. As the gilding can only be done in favourable weather, it is important that the amount should be raised at once, so that the order for the work may be given as soon as possible.

It was, and the work was done. Ingram Godfrey had given a new communion table in 1872, and John Richards presented a reredos in 1878. In 1886 Miss Godfrey gave a new organ—still in use more than a century later. The spire was restored (at a cost of £365) in 1883; the nave and north aisle were re-roofed and the south wall restored (£600) in 1895. Ingram Godfrey met the cost of rehanging the bells in 1886 and, three years later, paid for the land to enlarge the churchyard. In 1890 the last of the four galleries was taken down.

Richards was an undiscriminating moderniser and, on the introduction of gas lighting into the church in 1873, secured the removal of the great brass chandelier from the tower-crossing; in 1877 'the churchwardens were authorised to dispose of the old chandelier in any way which they might deem best', and it was sold in 1879 for £20 to William Oxenden Hammond, the Canterbury banker, for the hall of his new house at St Alban's Court, Nonington (where it still hangs). In 1875, 'the Vicar having represented that the Communion plate, and especially the flagon, was of a form very inconvenient for use, and suggested alterations, it was resolved that the Vicar and churchwardens be requested to consider some plan for remedying the inconvenience complained of'. The flagon, made in 1721 by one of the foremost English silversmiths, Anthony Nelme, in the greatest period of English silver, and a Georgian Communion cup of about 1756, were sold, and replaced by modern designs more to Richards' liking. (There was scathing criticism of the 'modern jug-shaped flagon' in *Archaeologia Cantiana* as early as 1886.) Perhaps because of his own modest beginnings, Richards was very conscious of his social position as vicar of the parish. He did not like the Georgian vicarage in Chequer Lane, bought in 1818 as the parsonage after incumbents had already lived in it for several years, and at his request it was sold in 1871. The 'handsome modern mansion in the style of the Renaissance' (built in 1856 for Captain Godden, part-owner of the Ash brewery, who was leaving the parish), in Sandwich Road next to the brewery, was bought in its place. This move was regretted by all Richards' successors, as 'a far more expensive house to maintain'. Worse, as a result of Richards' unfortunate decision to receive a payment of commuted tithe instead of a fixed stipend, the vicar's income fell (with the price of wheat) from £300 p.a. in 1875 to £254 by 1889 and to £215 by 1903.

Yet in 1888 an iron mission room at St Augustine's, Richborough was opened, followed in 1892 by another at Goldstone. At Westmarsh, Mrs. Rundell, the vicar's wife, arranged in 1889 for the erection of an iron room, to be used as a reading-room, at a cost of about £40. However, at Ash in 1899 a passing journalist reported with some astonishment that

> the church, except during the hours of public divine service appears to be rigorously closed and on the occasion of a recent visit we found it by no means an easy matter to secure admittance … This fact, as we took the liberty of hinting to one of the clergy, scarcely acts as an inducement to those who may desire a place for silent devotion … We were promptly met, however, by a rejoinder to the effect that people who did not go to church on Sundays were most unlikely to seek it on weekdays.

FIFTEEN

Ash before the First World War

Private Tapsell, from New Street, was one of those who took part in the historic charge by the 21st Lancers at Omdurman, on the bank of the Nile opposite the ruins of Khartoum, on 2 September 1898. In two minutes, the Lancers lost a fifth of their number: five officers, 65 men and 119 horses killed or wounded. Tapsell came through it all unscathed, and was back in Ash in January 1899.

There had been a sensation at Westmarsh in January 1898, when the licensee of the *Rose* set fire to it after killing his grandson, and then hanged himself. In May 1899, 40-year old Joseph Gifford was unloading bricks from a cart when the horse started and threw him out, so that a wheel passed right over his body. He died next day, leaving a widow and 10 children. In September 1899, while cycling on the Ramsgate road, the Walmer Royal Marines' chaplain ran against the roadside bank, was thrown under the wheels of a traction engine from Ash, and killed. At the inquest the driver of the engine was found in no way to blame. In the same month £100 was quickly subscribed in the village in aid of the Hougham, Thompson and Standing families whose thatched cottages in New Street had been destroyed by fire. In December, news reached Ash that the Godfreys' 36-year-old nephew, Captain Arthur Godfrey, serving in Zanzibar with the Duke of Wellington's West Riding Regiment, had been killed by a lion.

The Ash Athletic Association, the 'AAA', trained by a Royal Marine instructor from Walmer, was proficient enough to give displays of singlesticks and blind-boxing, and on the parallel bars, horizontal bar and vaulting horse, at Ash and Eastry Flower Shows. In April 1900, at the suggestion of James Sheppard, the assistant curate, it was decided to re-start an Ash Cricket Club, to play in Molland Meadow 'where, before cycling was so popular, an excellent cricket club existed'. Sheppard was also behind the formation in 1900 of an Ash company of the Church Lads' Brigade, for boys who had left school, were aged at least 14, and were members of the Church of England.

> Military drill is so popular just now that an organisation which brings this so prominently forward in its work should be as popular here as it is in hundreds of other parishes. The cap, worn with a belt and a white haversack, gives lads and young men a very smart appearance.

He was right, and the Ash company drilled, paraded at church, and marched enthusiastically. Sheppard got up a concert to buy rifles for the boys: 'It is probable the rifles will only fire *caps*, but they are useful for drilling with, and the various exercises with even a 'dummy' rifle are very useful in developing the muscles of the Brigade lads'. In May 1901 the Ash company even paid a memorable visit to London, where the boys, led by Sheppard, marched from Cannon Street to the Tower, from Westminster Bridge (reached by steamer) up Whitehall to Trafalgar Square, and then (after an adjournment to the London Hippodrome) to Charing Cross.

Fatal accidents occurred in the village on three successive Mondays in August and September 1901. While working on a threshing machine at Moat Farm, John Moore, aged 52, who had only come to Ash that day, was caught in the machinery; William Hodges, mounting the cab of a traction engine between Ash and Guilton, slipped and was run over and crushed; and nine-month-old James Scamp was killed at Westmarsh. The same day that the child died, William Deverson was thrown from the waggon he was driving, and injured. About a fortnight later, the sand gave way under two men clearing the top of the sandbank behind the *Lion Inn*, and threw them into the garden below. One of them, Hougham, was one of those whose homes in New Street had been burnt down two years earlier. In November there was a fourth fatality: James Twyman, 36, slipped while descending steps behind the *George and Dragon*, and was killed instantly, leaving a widow and six children. In July 1902, five-year-old Guy Norton disappeared the day after he had been on the annual Sunday School treat at Sandwich Bay, and his body lay undiscovered for five weeks in a clover field not far from his grandfather's home.

* * * *

The South African War broke out at the end of October 1899, and the vicar called a meeting on 9 November to consider how to aid sufferers in the war. A collection for the Lord Mayor's Fund raised over £100, including £40 from the Godfreys. 'On the common ground of citizenship of the Empire, all classes and denominations could, and did, co-operate', commented the *Parish Magazine*. Reservists were recalled to the colours, a recruiting office was established in The Street, and at least 13 men from Ash (including three White brothers from Richborough) were soon serving in South Africa. A concert, the first of several held in Ash, was arranged by the Misses Gwatkin of Elmstone Court in aid of war funds. 'Kipling's song, "The Absent-Minded Beggar" proved as popular here as it had proved elsewhere', the *Parish Magazine* reported,

> and as it had only been published as a song about a week, was a novelty. The appeal to 'Pay, Pay, Pay', by 'putting a little money in the little tambourine' was very liberally responded to by those present, a number of gold pieces appearing on the parchment when the tambourine came back to the platform. Major Gwatkin opened the entertainment by a telling little speech. Miss Evylyn Gwatkin's conjuring, and both the Misses Gwatkins' acting of a duologue, were very much appreciated.

The Cartwright School's headmaster, Herbert Webberley, sang 'Soldiers of the Queen', with chorus by all present. In church, a litany hymn was sung every Sunday evening, 'Guard our troops in foreign land, Help their courage long to stand: Strengthen every British hand, While we kneel and pray.' In May 1900 the *Parish Magazine* printed an account by an Ash man, Private Fox, serving with the 2nd Battalion of The Buffs, the East Kent Regiment, of the British victory at Klip Kraal Drift, and the capture of 4,500 Boers, followed in September by Corporal White's description of the battle at Biddulph's Berg. On Saturday, 19 May 1900, when news reached Ash of the relief of Mafeking after a 217-day siege, the church bells were rung, the village was 'be-flagged and be-decked, and a torchlight procession organised which marched from Guilton to Mr. Gardner's meadow'. Next month, the fall of Pretoria, the Boer capital, was the occasion for even greater rejoicing.

> Flags and flowers, and laurel-wreathed portraits of Lord Roberts made the village look gay in the day-time, and illuminations, fireworks, and a torch-light procession made it even gayer at night. The celebration of the event began early—at 5 a.m.—with a rousing peal of the church bells. … Another peal was rung at noon. The torchlight-procession was a great success. It was led by the village band. Then came the Volunteers. Then the Church Lads' Brigade, drawing a representation of the 'Long Toms' which did such execution at Ladysmith. Then came a very fine triumphal car, planned and driven by Mr. Cooke, of New Street. Soldiers and sailors surrounded John Bull, who surmounted the other groups of figures on the car. 'Mr. Kruger' had a back seat on the same car. An ambulance followed, with a mounted escort of people in coats of many colours, and 50 torch-bearers lit up the whole cavalcade.

A tin of chocolate, one of those given by Queen Victoria to every man serving in South Africa, was displayed in the window of Mr. Beer's fancy-goods shop in Ash.

> Mrs. Evans, who received it from her son in South Africa, kindly allowed it to be exhibited, but we are glad to say it is not for sale. A copy of the Queen's autograph with her good wishes, is stamped on each box, as well as a picture of the Queen herself. It would be scant courtesy to one's sovereign to sell the personal present she made to individual soldiers, so we are glad to find that in Ash, at all events, recipients of the Queen's gift appreciate it duly.

The war dragged on, and in August 1901 the *Parish Magazine* reported that Herbert Kelsey, a great-nephew of Thomas Kelsey who had founded the infants school 60 years earlier, had died, aged 22, while serving as a sergeant in the Imperial Yeomanry, from typhoid fever, 'which has killed far more of our men than the Boer bullets'. He had worked for three years at the brewery, and 'had taken a leading part in everything athletic while he lived here. He was a good "ringer", a prominent member of the gymnasium here, and far the best cricketer in the Ash Cricket Club.'

* * * *

In celebration of the postponed coronation of Edward VII, recovered from appendicitis, on 9 August 1902, after a church service (at which the Congregational minister read lessons, but did not otherwise take part),

> almost the whole village proceeded to the Molland Field where tea was served in a large marquee; including the children some 1,200 persons were thus entertained. The Ash brass band was in attendance, and its music was enjoyed by all. Sports of various kinds filled up the rest of the time, and a torchlight procession concluded the proceedings of the day. The village was beautifully illuminated.

63 Ash Sports Committee, 1901.

In June 1907 the annual Open Air Service in aid of the Kent & Canterbury Hospital was held in Moat Field. 'There was a large attendance, more than a thousand people being present. The Band of the Ramsgate East Kent Volunteers attended, and also the Drum and Fife Band of the Ash Company of C.L.B.' But at the same event in July 1910, as the procession reached Moat Field, the weather took a hand. 'Just at that moment the rain came down in a perfect torrent. It was quite impossible to hold any service at all. It is a great pity that on such occasions prejudice prevents the use of the Parish Church.'

When Robert Burgess looked back on visits to his grandfather Thomas Coleman at Goss Hall before 1914, he particularly remembered the farm scullery.

> It had a flagstone floor and three large built-in coppers, a big open fireplace and baking oven, and also a large stone sink with water supplied from a long-handled pump. In those days there was no main water supply, and a workman had to come into the scullery every morning to pump up water to the house storage tank in the roof. At the side of the scullery was a large box-like press which could be wound to and fro, and also an iron hand mangle. Adjoining the scullery was the creamery, with its cream separator and butter churn.

In the dining room, he admired the almost life-sized portraits of early Victorian ancestors in their massive gilt frames. He was thrilled to be able to sleep with his brother in a four-poster bed, but sad not to be allowed to draw the curtains round it at night. 'Ablutions

64   Mrs. Thomas Coleman of Goss Hall, in her carriage outside her home, *c*.1900.

with hot water necessitated the housemaids bringing up cans of hot water to bedrooms, or bathrooms where there were only hip baths.' There was no cesspool drainage, but only

> earth privies, in a brick hut at the end of a garden wall. In it were two self-contained privies, backing on to each other. The one for use by the domestic staff was approached outside the garden wall from the back scullery porch. The other, for family use, was approached from the front of the house on the garden side of the wall, down a short garden path screened by a holly hedge. Hence we had a euphemism for attending to the calls of nature, saying, 'I am going down the holly walk'. The holly-walk family privy was what was known as a three-holer: it had a throne with two large holes to seat adults, and a lower seat with a smaller hole for a child.

At this time the workmen at Gardner's brewery would walk down the village street to breakfast wearing clogs.

The village was beginning to expand. In 1898 the Sixteen-acre Field lying between Sandwich Road and New Street, part of Moat Farm, was sold in acre lots; and from 1903 building plots were sold at Guilton. In 1903 the Gardners built a terrace of four bungalows as almshouses at Resthaven in Sandy Lane; they replaced Elizabeth Godfrey's two small dark almshouses in the Cartwright School yard, and two lost almshouses adjoining the sub-post office. There was other building in Queen's Road—as Sandy Lane, or Gas House Lane, was re-named by the Parish Council in 1911—and on the east side of Chequer Lane. In all, 31 new houses were built between 1901 and 1911. But the population did not grow; it fell: from 2,242 in 1891 to 2,136 in 1901, and to 2,055 in 1911.

65 Gardner's Ash Ales, as advertised in the *Kentish Observer* for 19 January 1899.

GARDNER & Co.,

(LIMITED),

ASH BREWERY.

FAMILY BITTER ALE,

4½ Gallons } 4/3 & 4/9 { Cash on Delivery

Celebrated for its Delicacy of flavour and Tonic

Properties,

PORTER & STOUT,

4½ Gallons } 4/3 & 5/9 { Cash on delivery

Equal to the best London Brews.

Full Price List of all classes of Beer

on application

66 The workmen and boys at Gardner's Brewery, *c.*1899. The brewery was for many years the largest employer in the village.

67   Gardner's Brewery steam dray, *c.*1910.

In 1911 the possibility of building a village hall was discussed at a Church Vestry, and then at a public meeting held 'in connection with the celebration of the Coronation'. A site had already been found, and the new hall in Queen's Road, intended to meet 'the spiritual, intellectual, moral, social or political wants' of the parish, and built for £1,200, was opened in 1912. Ash Football Club was established by 1910. In 1912, 54 Ash men enlisted in the National Reserve, and a rifle range was fitted up in Reed Barn in Sandwich Road. The Ash & District Rifle Club was still in existence at least until 1924.

Established for 'the advancement of horticulture generally and especially among cottage gardeners', the Ash & District Horticultural & Cottage Gardeners' Society held its Flower Show annually from about 1894, with breaks only for the two Wars; first, for many years in Molland Meadow, before it was planted with cherries in 1935, and from about 1925 on the new Recreation Ground.

During Canterbury Cricket Week, in the years before 1914, the Woodruff, Harden and Saunders families would hire a horse-drawn omnibus to take them there from Ash, by way of Patrixbourne. About 1900 the new road bridge at Pluck's Gutter, replacing a passenger ferry, enabled some travellers to Thanet to avoid paying toll at Grove Ferry or Sandwich bridge. A passenger ferry from Red House, north of Paramour Street, operated until 1914. So did another, around 1900, from Richborough to the *Red Lion* at Stonar Cut, used by visitors to the Castle coming by horse-brake from Ramsgate. (Early in the 19th century, there had been a 'Keete Bridge', north of Rubery Drove, and during the First World War a timber footbridge from Potts Farm Drove was built across the river to Minster.)

68 Ash Football XI, in White Post Meadow, 1910.

69 The maypole, at Ash Flower Show in Molland Meadow, 1902.

70 The East Kent Light Railway; the first train at Ash Town Halt, 18 April 1913. The 0-4-0 saddle-tank engine, built by Andrew Barclay & Sons, Kilmarnock, had been bought second-hand.

71 One of the first motor-buses to serve the village: Deal & District Motor Services had started a regular twice-daily service between Deal and Canterbury in 1910. This Daimler, DU4529, with an American-designed 'Silent Knight' engine, built in Coventry in 1914, was fitted with a 24-seater charabanc body.

Ash did not escape the 'coal fever' which swept through east Kent. In August 1913 work began on the 'Fleet Boring', near Fleet Farm. Chalk was reached at 85 feet, and the coal measures at 1,089 feet; boring stopped in December at a depth of 1,966 feet. Ever optimistic, the report was that 'although a number of seams of no commercial value were met with ... there are several of nice workable thickness within easy striking distance. Analyses show all these seams to be of excellent quality, giving every promise of proving highly remunerative to work.' Many, perhaps most, owners of farmland leased the coal beneath it, hoping for royalties when mining began. The East Kent Light Railway, constructed as part of the development of the Kent coalfield, joined Wingham and Shepherdswell, with a branch to Richborough. Parts of the line opened to goods traffic in 1913, and from 1916 passengers were carried. Ash Town Halt, accessible only on foot, was south of Pudding Lane; Staple Station was in Durlock Road; Moat Farm and Poulton each had its own private siding. Already in 1910, Deal & District Motor Services had extended their motor-bus service through Ash to Canterbury.

* * * *

Wooden 'one-way' Kentish ploughs, which swivelled from one side of their beam to the other—enabling furrows to be laid alternately left and right, so that all sloped in one direction leaving the ploughed land level, without an open furrow between ridges—were still in use at Molland until 1914, and at Goldstone Court until the 1930s. John Spanton of Molland remembered:

> Men had to be out in the stable at 6 a.m. There were nine horses here; the waggoner and his mate had two horses each; the next stable was the second man's and the second boy's. The waggoner would lead them up into the fields. They'd 'go one yoke' from 6 until 2 in the afternoon. Then they'd go home and have their dinner, come back and clean their horses, chop the food for them, and litter them down. Then they'd go home at 5 o'clock. The second man and second boy would come and bait the horses at 8 o'clock: they had to put an hour in, water them and feed them for the night. At 4 o'clock in the morning the waggoner and second man used to come down, muck the horses out, and give them their breakfast. Then they used to go home, call the mate and the second boy, have breakfast, and be out in the fields at 6 o'clock, winter as well as summer.

A man who began work as a boy of 13 in 1914, on a farm where his father was the waggoner, also looked back

> We worked from six in the morning till half past five, six days a week. My wages were 6d. a day. Next year I was waggoner's mate: wages £3 a year, and mother was paid 4s. 6d. a week for my keep. I must have been one of the last to work on a Michaelmas hiring like that; no wages until you'd worked the whole year, and if you left during the year nothing at all. As waggoner's mate I had to go back at 8 o'clock in the evening to bait the horses. Father had to be at the stable every morning to give the horses their breakfast, but when he stopped at half past 5 in the afternoon, he'd finished for the day. I stuck it out on a yearly hiring for two years. Then I'd had enough; when I was nearly 17 I became a weekly labourer, paid 8s. a week. Two years later I was 'second man'. A waggoner had a team of four horses to look after; a second man only had a pair. But a second man had no mate, so I had to feed my horses myself at

4 o'clock every morning, and again at eight every evening. If you were 10 minutes late in the morning, you had to 'lose a quarter', and wait until 9 o'clock to start work. You had to put up with it; there were plenty of others ready to take your job. But it wasn't so bad; we were happy enough. You hardly ever had to pay any rent, because you could work it off by putting in a few extra hours. We got free milk, and often free fat pork to help with boarding the men. Mother would have up to four men living in with us: she got 4s. 6d. a week for each of them, or 4s. if the governor provided pork. I'm only a little chap, but I could manage sacks of wheat or peas, weighing two and a quarter hundredweight; carry them up ladders, too. The day I was 19, I carried 30 quarters of barley up a ladder at Walmer brewery.

The Ash Sparrow Club, founded in 1888 as the 'Ash and Staple Sparrow Club', met monthly in winter at the *Lion*. Each member had to take or send 'not less than 24 heads per month, or forfeit one half-penny per head for all deficient; Linnets, Chaffinches, Bullfinches and Starlings to count as Sparrows'. (By 1933, when it was the 'Ash & District Rat & Sparrow Club', bounty was paid for sparrows' heads and eggs, rats' and moles' tails, and queen wasps.)

John Spanton remembered:

When we were school kids, Mother used to go to Dover to shop, or to Hunts at Canterbury, and buy all our school rig-outs, and that sort of thing. And we only paid the bill once a year, when we got the hop cheques. Mother used to take a cheque up, and old Mr. Hunt he'd say, 'Mrs. Spanton, if it wasn't for you country people, we couldn't exist.' But they had to carry us for twelve months.

Yet his father, Troward Spanton, was the first in Ash to own a motor-car, a 24/40 h.p. Minerva, with no hood or windscreen, about 1909, when petrol cost 11d. a gallon from the village chemist.

* * * *

The newly arrived assistant curate, James Sheppard, an energetic Irishman, had started a *Parish Magazine* in January 1899, selling 400 copies a month at 1d. each. The Ash and Westmarsh branch of the Mothers' Union, formed in 1898, had some 90 members by the end of 1899. Farmers' waggons carried 218 children on the annual Sunday School Treat in 1899, held as usual by the sea at the Coastguard Battery. But the elderly vicar, Edward Woods, retired at the end of October 1901 and, as was the custom, his curate, Sheppard, also left the parish. The new vicar, Francis Michell, returned from India several years previously, where he had been Archdeacon of Calcutta, took himself and his duties very seriously. His complaint in August 1902 that 55 children had been born in the parish in 1901, but only 29 had been baptised in the parish church, was the first of many to his parishioners about their slackness, delivered with depressing and deadening frequency in the *Parish Magazine*. He could not laugh at himself. His handwriting was often indecipherable, but in May 1903 he wrote: 'The list of candidates confirmed, which appeared in our last number, contains we are sorry to say, two bad mistakes. We beg to apologise for them, and cannot understand how they occurred. For Ernest Albert *Gritton*, read E.A. Sutton; and for Arthur George *Clegsman*, read A.G. Chapman.' He was

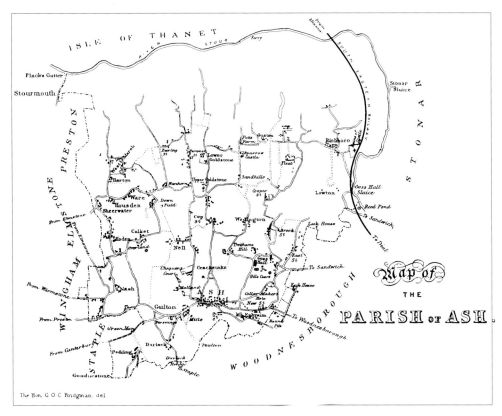

72 The parish of Ash in 1864 (drawn by the Hon. G.O.C. Bridgeman, later 4th Earl of Bradford (1845-1915), while a pupil at Ash Vicarage).

over-anxious that nothing should diminish his position in the parish. In September 1903 he wrote:

> The old Billiard Room in the Vicarage has been put in thorough order … It has often been called the 'Parish Room', but quite wrongly so for it is part of the Vicarage House, and has to be maintained and kept in repair entirely at the Vicar's charge. It is useful, however, that it should have a name, and certainly it would not be appropriate to call it the Billiard Room. It will, therefore, in future be known as 'The Vicar's Room'.

In 1907 William Dixon, the chemist, retired as church organist after 52 years' service, and at the Harvest Festival that year the church choir were robed in surplices for the first time. Churchgoing was still a social occasion. Robert Burgess recalled how

> On Sundays, [our nursemaid] dressed us in our best sailor suits and we were driven by Dunster [the Colemans' coachman] in great pomp, with granny, to Ash church. I remember thinking that Dunster ought to have a cockade on his hat, like that on the hat of the local squire's coachman. Old Squire Godfrey sat opposite us in church, and on one occasion we got into trouble for giggling when his top hat rolled into the aisle during the sermon.

Sixteen

THE FIRST WORLD WAR,
AND AFTERWARDS

War was declared on Tuesday, 4 August 1914. 'On Thursday evening', the *Parish Magazine* reported,

> a Recruiting Meeting was held in the Cartwright Schoolroom. Although only 24 hours' notice had been given the room was full. Captains Hendry and Dallas were there and spoke, also Sergeant Major Cullen from Woodnesborough. The result was that 22 men volunteered. Dr. McCall Smith and Major Baylor (late A.M.C.), who were present, examined them. Two were found to be under age, and therefore not eligible. The rest were passed. A motor was sent into Sandwich and the Mayor fetched up to swear them in, and by 8 a.m. the next morning all were on their way to join a depot as recruits.

73   Technical education at the Cartwright School, *c.*1925: the headmaster Mr. Webberley's gardening class.

74 Ash Village Hall: the Voluntary Aid Detachment hospital, *c.*1915. Some of the local VADs, with their patients, wounded soldiers, many of them Belgians.

Soon the East Kent Light Railway was in use by trains carrying troops on their way to France. On 26 October a driver of the 1st Home Counties Brigade 2nd Battery RFA sent a postcard home from Ash Town Halt, 'We are going on board Wednesday and sail Friday'.

The new Village Hall was quickly offered as an emergency 20-bed VAD hospital. At a public meeting on 8 August, volunteers came forward to offer cash, beds, and furniture. By May 1915, it had been enlarged to 26 beds, and all were full with wounded men from the front in Belgium and France, with several Canadians among them. In October 1917 the Commandant, Mrs. Winsome, wrote in the *Parish Magazine*,

> May I take this opportunity to thank all those who have so generously contributed gifts in kind to the VAD Hospital, and at the same time make a special appeal for contributions in cash, as at the present our 'Detachment Fund' is low, from which source all upkeep and the salary of our trained sister is drawn. The 3s. War Office grant per day per patient has to pay for everything else. I am sure all interested in the Hospital will hope to keep the flag flying until the end of the War.

Officers and men of the Suffolk Yeomanry, the West Lancashire Field Artillery, the South Notts Hussars (September 1916-April 1917) and the 2/1st Derbyshire Yeomanry (December 1917) were successively billeted at Ash. The farm buildings at Molland were requisitioned; officers were billeted in the farmhouse, and the men camped under canvas in the meadow. Troward Spanton bought horses on commission for the Army, 60 or 70 at a time, and from Molland sent them over to France.

In 1916 'Guilton Aerodrome' was laid out on 25 acres of grassland east of Overland Lane, with a staff of two airmen billeted at Overland Farm, a wooden hut and a windsock, as an emergency landing-ground for No. 50 Home Defence Squadron RFC, based from 1915 at Bekesbourne to intercept raiding Zeppelins. It was guarded by three 13-pdr field guns. The duty airman had to put out acetylene lamps round a chalk circle and move a T-shaped tarpaulin as the wind changed, to show pilots of aeroplanes where and in which direction to land. (Sixty years later, the hut was still there, and the chalk circle could still be seen when the land was freshly worked.)

Land occupied by Troward Spanton at Stonar was requisitioned, and from September 1916 Richborough Port was created, covering 2,200 acres and containing 65 miles of railway. It was the centre of the cross-Channel barge service, carrying ammunition to France, as well as hay, vehicles and air-force supplies. Its five yards together held 3,265 railway-wagons. Barges were built on 22 slipways; and in February 1918 three 3,650-ton train-ferries went into service, carrying tanks and heavy guns to Calais and Dunkirk. By the end of the War, the barges—mostly of 180 tons capacity, but some holding 1,000

75 The donkey carriage, in Chequer Lane, *c*.1915, belonged to Miss Gardner of Guilton Rectory, who lent it for use by wounded soldiers on the road to recovery.

76 Hop-picking, with convalescent soldiers helping out, in Marchant's hop-garden at Guilton, *c.*1915.

77 Women working on the land, manning a reaper and binder, perhaps about 1918.

tons—had made over 20,000 trips across the Channel. The Port lay mostly in Minster and Sandwich, but Richborough Yard, a railway marshalling yard, and a construction camp and stores depot, as well as the guard room and a 10-cell detention block (still standing, semi-derelict, in 1990), and Richborough Military Halt, built in 1917 on the South Eastern & Chatham Railway beneath Richborough Castle, were all in Ash parish.

In the *Parish Magazine*, Michell, the 75-year-old vicar, repeatedly urged upon the parish the need for more volunteers to join up. In December 1914 he wrote, 'Can it be said that our able-bodied men whose duty it is to protect the Fatherland, have come forward as they should have done? The call at this moment for a million more men is clear proof that the response to the national call to arms has not so far received the answer it demands.' When Mrs. Pettit of Ware Farm received a letter from the king congratulating her on the fact she had five sons and two sons-in-law fighting in France, Michell commented 'This is a noble example of loyalty to the young men in this district. God speed all those who follow in their steps, and then nobly do their duty. It is to be hoped that there are now no "slackers" in East Kent—none, hereafter, to be looked upon as cowards.' When conscription came in February 1916 he wrote, 'If at such a crisis as this any man refuses to take part in the defence of his King and Country he is surely not fit to be called an Englishman.' During May 1917, 156 parcels were despatched from the Ash Gifts and Comforts Fund to men on active service.

On 30 September 1917 the evening Harvest Festival service at Westmarsh was interrupted by an air raid. 'Although the guns could be plainly heard, and the whistling of the shells seemed too near to be pleasant, there was no restiveness, and a hearty service was brought to an end as usual by singing the Vesper Hymn. There was still heavy firing as the villagers returned to their homes.' When, as churchwarden, Austen Gardner advised Emmanuel College of damage to the windows on the north side of the Molland chancel in Ash church, he blamed gunfire.

Farmers prospered during the war, despite the requisitioning of their land and shortages of labour, and Troward Spanton, Clarence Quested of Poulton and Thomas Coleman of Goss Hall went into partnership and bought the East Kent Brewery at Sandwich and the Sandwich Hoy Company.

But in January 1917 Michell wrote,

> From our small parish … we have sent over 200 men into the Army and Navy. Some of these men have already laid down their lives, others have been wounded and some have been invalided home; and, what is perhaps saddest of all, some are missing and their nameless graves will probably never be known.

In March 1917 a Roll of Honour of the men from Ash serving in the armed forces was unveiled outside the Village Hall on which 'the fallen have the word "Promoted" written after their name'. Before 1917 was out the number of men serving had risen to some 300, of whom 20 were known to have died (in fact, the true figure was at least 40). By the end of the War, the number of men from the parish who had been killed or had died on active service was 58. Of the 57 certainly identified, the first (a former master at the Cartwright School) was killed in September 1914 in the battle of the Aisne, and the last died of pneumonia on 10 November 1918, the day before the Armistice. Two died in 1914, 11 in 1915, 8 in 1916, 18 in 1917 and 18 in 1918. Two were in the Royal Navy;

78   This closed carriage belonged to the brewer, Austen Gardner of Guilton Rectory. It is seen here standing in Chequer Lane in 1922, outside the Kelsey Infants School (demolished *c*.1965)

79   E. Jacobs & Son's East Kent (Cash) Stores: Ironmongery, Furnishings, Grocery and Provisions; Pratt's Motor Spirit, *c*.1925. Victor Jacobs, is seen with his staff and a Model-T Ford delivery van.

80   Mowing at Goss Hall, *c.*1930.

81   Carting at Goss Hall, *c.*1930.

82   Guilton Corner, *c*.1920.

two were airmen; and the remainder were soldiers: one dying in India, three at Gallipoli, 32 on the Western Front, and two as prisoners of war in Germany. On the new War Memorial in The Street at Ash, dedicated in May 1920, 45 names were inscribed, and 13 more on the Memorial at Westmarsh church.

After the war ended Richborough Port was still busy. Almost 400,000 tons of salvage were brought back from France to sidings north-east of Richborough Castle, and there sorted by some 800 girls brought in daily by train to Richborough Military Halt. In January 1919 the Parish Council was calling for the re-opening of the Sandwich–Ramsgate road to civilian traffic. In the same month, the War Office handed the Village Hall back to the trustees.

The last windmill in Ash, a tarred post-mill on Mount Ephraim, dated 1735 but moved by Zechariah Hudson from Coombe or Ringleton about 1818 (when it was said to have been drawn to Mount Ephraim by 16 oxen), ceased to grind bread-flour about 1918, but continued to make animal and poultry foods for another ten years. One day in 1918 the miller, Joseph Brockman, was working in the 'roundhouse', the store at the base

83   The last windmill at Guilton, *c.*1934, drawn by Donald Maxwell (1877-1936).

of the mill, when he heard the revolving sweeps 'bumping'. Going out, he discovered 14-year old Rose Beer, from New Street, who had been sent to buy grain, lying unconscious with a fractured skull, and critically ill. The village doctor, Dr. McCall Smith, held out little hope of her recovery, but she did survive and lived until 1946. In July 1920, as Selina Brockman, the 64-year old miller's wife, emerged from the roundhouse, she too was struck by the revolving sweeps. She died from her injuries a few days later.

There had been other windmills in the parish. A map of 1736 showed a windmill north-west of Knell Farm. At Guilton, there were two mills, one a post-mill, about 1840, three in 1854, and only one, a smock-mill, by 1872, which was demolished, but for its base, in 1933. About 1840, and perhaps long before, Hudson operated a second post-mill in Ash, sited on the edge of a sandpit north of the *Lion*, which had gone before 1872. Good Intent Mill (or Carter's Mill), a post-mill west of Chequer Lane, was pulled down about 1905.

In 1920 Thomas Coleman resigned from his partnership with Clarence Quested and Troward Spanton. He was lucky. Shortly afterwards, at 2.30 a.m. on Sunday, 15 August, the partners' two-masted Thames spritsail hoy, the *Dorcas*, left the Anglo-American Oil Company's Silvertown wharf in the Port of London, bound for Sandwich with a cargo of 22,500 gallons of petrol. At 3.15 a.m. there was an explosion; the skipper was killed, and the crew of two went overboard. The drifting ship, ablaze from stem to stern, hit the Woolwich Ferry pontoon, and set it and a ferry alight. In a widening pool of burning oil, craft after craft caught fire. At 4 a.m. the *Dorcas* blew up, throwing flames 300 feet into the air, and three fire engines were engulfed in the inferno. At the subsequent enquiry, it was supposed that the skipper must have lit his pipe and dropped the lighted match through a crack in a hatch. Either the partners' insurance cover was insufficient or their insurers would not pay. The claims ruined both Quested and Spanton.

Kelly's *Directory* for 1918 listed 'E. Smith & P.G. Armstrong, motor engineers' at Ash, but John Ayling, very long established, was still listed as 'building repairs, sanitary engineer, decorator, coach-painter, undertaker, carpenter, wheelwright, garage proprietor, cars and cycles for hire and repair'. However, besides 'E. Smith, Lion Garage, Ash', the 1923 Michelin Guide listed 'Ayling & Bourn, Central Garage, High St., Ash, Telephone 39X4, open on Sundays', with a garage big enough for six cars, an inspection pit, electric plant for charging accumulators, and two cars for hire.

The Ash Girl Guide Company was formed in 1919, one of the earliest in Kent. In 1924 Hamilton Godfrey of Brooke House gave four acres of land in Queen's Road as a recreation ground, in memory of his son William John Godfrey, killed in France in 1916 at the age of 19, when serving as a subaltern in The Black Watch. Fundraising in Westmarsh enabled a timber village hall to be erected at Ware in 1929. By the early 1930s a Bowling Club and a Lawn Tennis Club had been formed with rink and courts in Moat Lane.

The Primitive Methodist chapel at Cooper Street closed in 1937. In the parish church the bells were re-hung in 1927, and two re-cast; in 1937-8 the organ was moved from the Molland chancel into the south transept, and the pulpit from beneath the central tower and the choir stalls from the high chancel, and electric light (£130) was installed. The vicarage, the burdensome 'mansion' in Sandwich Road, was sold at last in 1938.

In 1928 Eastry Rural District Council bought seven acres of land in Chequer Lane from Emmanuel College, on which subsidised houses were built, first privately and then by the Council itself. More houses were built at Guilton and in Chequer Lane, Queen's Road and New Street. Plans for a colliery village on Richborough hill received a set-back when the District Council disapproved of back-to-back dwellings, and only six houses were built, in Richborough Castle Road. In the end, the 'Fleet Colliery' was never constructed. Nor did the coal traffic for which the East Kent Light Railway had been built ever materialise; it had to manage with market-garden produce, and did not prosper. Southern Railway's Richborough Military Halt, closed in 1922, re-opened for public use as 'Richborough Castle Halt' in 1933, but closed finally in September 1939.

The Smallholdings and Allotments Act 1908, passed during the farming depression

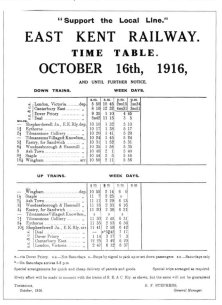

84 East Kent Light Railway timetable, 1916. Passengers were not carried until 1916. Passenger traffic ceased in October 1948, and goods traffic in July.

85   The 'Second Ash Band', 1925.

ASH VICARAGE

Welcome to the

Annual Garden Party

On TUESDAY, AUGUST 11th

to be opened at 3 p.m. by

The Viscountess Hawarden

STALLS, of useful Articles, Eatables, Etc.

AMUSING SIDE SHOWS

including

Cokernut Shies, Aerial Railway, Chinese Washing, Etc.,

TEAS.   ICES.   REFRESHMENTS.

SCENES FROM SHAKESPEARE'S
"Much Ado About Nothing."

(Kind arranged by Mrs. Whinney ; Orchestra under
the direction of Mrs. Coleman)

Benedick—D. McCall Smith	Balthasar—E. Spinner
Leonato—H. Blacklocks	Beatrice—Elaine Crooks
Don Pedro—A. Dubosc	Hero—Margaret Archer
Claudio—D. V. Whinney	Usula—Gay Barton

THE ASH BAND
will play afternoon and evening
DANCING ON THE GREEN

ADMISSION :

3 p.m. to 5 p.m. 6d. After 5 p.m. and
Children 3d.

Proceeds for Parsonages Repairs Fund and
the Archbishop's Fund for promoting Religious Education in the Diocese.

86   The Vicarage Garden Party, 1931, as advertised
in the *Parish Magazine*.

which had lasted since the 1870s, was intended to give farm labourers a better chance of securing a small-farm tenancy. At Ash, the County Council bought two farms, Nash Court (before 1914) and Overland (about 1935), divided them up so as to form Shrub Cottage (later Greenland), Finchley, and Kingsland Farms, put up standardised houses and buildings (demolishing a fine 18th-century house at Overland), and let them all, later re-distributing some of the land. The project was finally abandoned, and all were sold, in the early 1990s.

The Ash & District branch of the NFU organised the first East Kent Fruit Show in the Village Hall in October 1927, at which several classes were open only to growers within eight miles of Ash village. It soon outgrew the Village Hall, and moved to Sandwich in 1932.

Farm workers' wages went up from on average of 16s. 4d. in 1910 to 25s. after 1918,

87 Ash Flower Show programme, 1926.

88 Ash Ladies Hockey Club, c.1935.

and later to 32s. 'A waggoner got 34s. then, but really he wasn't so well paid, because he had to do so much longer hours for his money.' But during the depression of the 1920s and '30s some of the large tenant farmers found it difficult even to pay their rent. 'We used to do a lot of bartering,' recalled John Spanton. 'Things got so bad there was no money about. Eggs were about 7½d. a dozen: they were the wife's perks; she used to run two or three hundred chicken. She used to pay for the groceries out of that, and what was left was hers.' He had a small dairy herd at Molland, with a milk round in the village.

> The surplus milk I used to take to Deal to sell wholesale, 23 miles, in the dickey of my Morris car. I used to do the round myself when my roundsman was laid up, about four miles. The milk round used to go off about 8 o'clock, or half past, but didn't get back until 1 o'clock or 2. But you'd never get your money, that was the trouble. Some of them, they didn't mean to pay.

In June 1934 Weddington Farm—80½ acres, with house, buildings and two cottages—was sold at auction for £3,400, just over £42 an acre. At the same sale, Moat Farm—112 acres, manor house, buildings, and six cottages—attracted no bid beyond £2,450, less than £22 an acre, and was unsold.

In the 1930s a number of Ash farmers joined the campaign for the abolition of tithes. Stewart Chandler took exception to having to pay to support an established church to which he did not belong, and in June 1936 he set off, with Gerald and Fred

89   The dairy herd at Guston Farm, 1928. The farm had a shop in Harnet Street, Sandwich. 'Pure cooled milk from our own cows, supplied in bottles if required. Devonshire produce fresh Tuesdays and Fridays. New Zealand honey, Maypole margarine, Kardomah teas, coffee and cocoa. Inspection of dairy and cowsheds invited.'

90 Molland Farm's milk roundsman, *c.*1935. White Post Farm also had a milk round.

Stickells of Great Ware Farm, with hoes, to demonstrate, processing through the streets of London to a rally in Hyde Park. That was not Gerald Stickells' only grievance. Much of the parish remained copyhold land, a good deal of it held directly of the manor of Wingham, each property liable to a tiny yearly quit-rent, until the 1930s when it was compulsorily 'enfranchised'. (Curiously, three of the Ash manors subordinate to Wingham— Goldstone, Goss Hall and Overland—had been the subject of separate 18th-century private Acts of Parliament, each passed to deal with a problem of aristocratic inherit- ance.) In February 1937 Stickells appeared in Canterbury County Court to answer a summons in respect of £14 12s. 6d. quit-rent due to Viscountess Hawarden as lord of the manor of Wingham. He claimed it had formerly been payable in kind or personal service, and offered to discharge it by handing over 10,000 cabbages or 300 bushels of apples. On another occasion, answering a similar summons, he questioned the Court's jurisdiction, pointing out that Lady Hawarden had claimed for land belonging to seven different owners, and did not seem to know what she was charging for. The duties of a lord of the manor had lapsed, so payments of quit-rent should also stop. 'It's such things as this', he said, 'that turn law-abiding citizens into Communists and Fascists.' Giving judgment for the amount claimed with costs, the judge told Stickells he could appeal if he was dissatisfied. 'I can't afford to do that', he replied, 'I don't want to stand a man off.'

Seventeen

The Second World War

On the outbreak of war in September 1939, 4,000 children were evacuated from the Medway towns—10s. 6d. a week was paid for the keep of each billeted child—and as late as March 1940 Ash was considered a safe reception area. Until the Village Hall could be pressed into service, Winifred Tower converted her dining room at Memories (now Mulberry House) in Chequer Lane into a schoolroom. The centre of Manston airfield was less than six miles from Ash village, and RAF Manston was transferred from Training Command to Fighter Command, part of 11 Group and controlled from the Hornchurch sector station, but about the most exciting local event to occur was the belly-landing in an orchard at Wingham Barton in January 1940 of a Fairey Battle bomber, which had suffered engine failure in a snowstorm.

But suddenly, with the end of the 'phoney war', everything changed. On 9 April the Germans invaded Denmark and Norway; on 10 May they invaded Holland, Belgium and Luxembourg, and Churchill became Prime Minister. On 14 May the Dutch army surrendered. That evening, on 'the wireless' after the 9 o'clock news, Eden, the Minister of War, announced the immediate mustering of 'Local Defence Volunteers'. Nineteen-year-old Robert Chandler cycled up the same evening from Goldstone to the police houses in Chequer Lane, to join, and he was not alone. On 16 May the BBC broadcast warnings against parachutists, and next day some of the new volunteers, wearing 'LDV' armbands but with very few rifles, were on patrol.

At Staple Station on the East Kent Light Railway on 18 May, the RAF began to take delivery of materials to construct a dummy airfield on Goldstone marshes, to divert raiding aircraft from the real airfield at Manston. 'A flashing light on top of a 4-wheeled trailer, towed around at night', was later replaced by fixed lights on buried cables fed by a generator.

Between 27 May and 4 June, against all odds, 338,000 troops, 224,000 of them from the BEF, were evacuated from the beaches of Dunkirk. Tim Winter from Walmestone (awarded a Military Cross), Ivan Castle from Guilton, William Lawrence from Goldstone and Harry Epps from The Street were not among them, and were taken prisoner. For his bravery during the evacuation, Harry Wellard from Poulton, who had worked for Arthur Marchant at Guilton, and was serving in the 1,250-ton sloop HMS *Pelican*, was awarded the Conspicuous Gallantry Medal—a rare decoration; only 72 CGMs were awarded during the war.

91   When the invader comes, 1940. The local Home Guard contingent was practising advancing down 'a village street, somewhere in south-east England'.

92   Members of the Ash Home Guard at Guilton, 1940. Crouching down with home-made petrol bombs, they were ready to meet the first German armoured columns—if they came.

The Ministry of Agriculture warned that 'unless military action in the immediate neighbourhood makes it impossible, farmers and farmworkers must go on ploughing, sowing, cultivating, hoeing and harvesting as though no invasion was occurring'. All civil responsibilities were to be given to a parish 'Invasion Committee' (in Ash, it was James Ogilvie, the doctor, Winifred Tower, and Albert Smith, clerk to the Parish Council) which was required to keep a 'War Book', containing such information as 'sites earmarked for mass graves', and to be destroyed 'should hasty evacuation become necessary'. Invasion was daily expected. Beach defences at Sandwich Bay included a mine barrage below high-water mark, and anti-tank barriers of tubular scaffolding and barbed-wire. Back from the beaches, there were demolition lines across the roads, to delay the invaders, and provision for demolishing Sandwich bridge and the port cranes at Richborough. Poles were erected in the fields, to prevent aircraft or gliders landing. Ash village was a 'Type B Nodal Point', intended to hold up the invaders for two days. Road blocks were set up in the main street outside the church and at Guilton; the junction with Chequer Lane was 'cratered'; and three machine-gun posts were formed: at the *Lion*, in the stables at Memories, and at Guilton Farm. The Ash LDV contingent's original HQ was at the old vicarage in Sandwich Road. Renamed

93   Old-style harvesting in 1940. The binder, first used in England in 1879, cut the corn and tied it with 'binder-twine' into sheaves which were thrown aside, ready to stand in shocks to dry until fit to carry and build into stacks to await the threshing machine.

the Home Guard, it later moved to two Nissen huts, one serving as an ammunition store, in the sandpit next to the Village Hall. At first the only weapon at its Cop Street post was a 12-bore shotgun. A group photograph includes five officers, nine NCOs and 30 men, their campaign medals showing that at least six had served in the First World War. Sergeant Stock, a drayman at the brewery, who held the China Medal, was believed to be at least seventy.

Ash village was just within the 3-mile coastal strip—temporarily extended to 10 miles in the spring of 1944—to which access was controlled for much of the remainder of the war. Passes had to be shown at the checkpoint at Guilton.

Manston airfield itself was only defended by 3-inch anti-aircraft guns dating from 1914-18 and a makeshift armoured car mounting a Lewis gun. Although it was no longer safe to base fighters there, it still seemed a perfect refuelling, re-arming and feeding post for squadrons from other stations detailed to protect shipping in the Channel and the Thames. But Manston was less than thirty miles from the coast of France, so that there was now not enough warning of an impending attack. Enemy aircraft flew at 20,000 feet, and unless defending fighters were already in the air, they could not gain height quickly enough. The first heavy raid occurred on 12 August; from then on, the airfield was repeatedly bombed and machine-gunned, and many aircraft were destroyed on the ground. Worst of all, on 24 August, damage was so severe that thick smoke obscured the vision of a second wave of bombers which as a result dropped many bombs on Ramsgate's civil aerodrome and the town. That day Manston effectively ceased to be an airfield of 11 Fighter Group, and thereafter served only as an emergency landing ground. Stories leaked out, swiftly denied but persistent, of a 'Manston mutiny' born of paralysing panic among ground crew caught in the raids. On 28 August Churchill himself visited Manston. He was concerned that 'although more than four clear days have passed since it was last raided, the greater part of the craters on the landing ground remained unfilled and the aerodrome was barely serviceable', and protested against 'this feeble method of repairing damage'.

Manston had the unenvied distinction of being the most bombed airfield in the United Kingdom, and much of what happened there could be clearly seen and heard from Ash. Many of the bombs which fell in the parish during the war, on at least nine separate occasions between September 1940 and January 1941 alone, luckily without any loss of life, were the result of German attacks targeted on Manston.

On Sunday morning, 25 August, the day following that worst attack on Manston, the sound of a heavy explosion could be clearly heard in the parish. At Sandwich Bay, Major Lord North, heir to the Earl of Guildford, his wife, and his sister Lady Cynthia Williams, intent on picnicking on the beach below their house, had wandered into a minefield. He and his sister were killed instantly, and his wife was critically injured.

In May 1940 a national network of about twenty 'Auxiliary Units', each with an officer and about twelve men, had been set up, supported by small 'patrols' composed of members of the local Home Guard, mostly single men without dependants, chosen for their resourcefulness and knowledge of the country, and intended to be left behind enemy lines as saboteurs after the invaders had passed through. The Ash patrol, in 'Grape Area', was 'Marrow Patrol'; John Marchant, Arthur Benbow and, later, Robert Chandler, were among its members. Its first 'Operational Base', into which they would have retired if

94 New-style harvesting in 1940, this time using a tractor, but the binder was unchanged.

the enemy had made a successful landing, was dug by the Army in the sandpit at Coombe. When, later, it began to collapse, members of the patrol constructed another at Ringleton—where they had problems not only with the sand but also with badgers— by burying an Anderson shelter, with concrete tubes and sandbags as an access tunnel. They were amused when an inspecting officer who complained that it wasn't well enough camouflaged, promptly stepped back into a concealed trench.

Illustrated magazine for 5 April 1941 included a set of photographs, designed to impress its readers (particularly, it is said, those in the USA) with the Home Guard's high level of morale and preparedness. In fact, nearly all the photographs were of the Ash contingent, presumably taken some weeks earlier, showing the men in battledress, all with steel helmets, gas mask cases, bandoliers, and HG brassards, mostly with greatcoats, and armed with American P-14 rifles. Several shots had been taken in the centre of the village; one of two men preparing a road block by inserting a short length of railway line into a socket in the roadway outside the church; another of six men at Guilton, one armed with a sub-machine gun, two with rifles, and three preparing to throw 'Molotov cocktails', home-made petrol-filled bottles. They were described as 'having attained a state of efficiency that is unsurpassed by any other Home Guard unit. Not a man among them would not be capable of taking his place in the front line.' Indeed, they might have had to do so. The original German plans for Operation 'Sea Lion', the invasion of England, only abandoned in late August 1940, did involve a sea-borne attack on Sandwich Bay and the low coastal strip between Ramsgate and Deal. (Not everything always went smoothly for the Ash Home Guard: on one occasion two members, one an officer, were, for some misdemeanour, formally stripped of their badges of rank.)

At the end of June 1940, 'B' Battery 74th Medium Regt RA had arrived at Brooke House, with 16 tractors dragging eight 60-pounder Mark 1 guns, last fired in the First World War (and said to have been retrieved from an open-air museum in Scotland). They were big: 5-inch calibre, 13 feet 4 inches long, and weighing 39 hundredweight. The battery had 160 shells for them, believed to be all that still existed. Four guns were dug into shallow pits and camouflaged alongside the narrow road north of Brooke House, to cover Pegwell Bay, well within their 10,000 yard range. The seven officers were accommodated in Brooke House itself; some of the 63 men were bedded down in the oast and the hoppers' huts, the rest had to stay under canvas. Joan Ogilvie, who had 'called' at Brooke House in 1938 as a newly-wed, and remembered the faded elegance of the Godfreys' drawing room, was startled now to find it stripped, and the walls covered by pin-ups. Later, some of the officers were billeted in the village and, with their wives, were invited by the Ogilvies to dances at Chilton House. The men of the battery were entertained, too, in other ways. One village girl claimed that among them was the father of the child she was expecting. All were paraded at Brooke House for her, but she finally said she couldn't decide which of them it had been because he'd 'had his hat on, at the time'. Some of the men, issued with rifles so as to be able to defend their guns, were taken to the range by the sea at Kingsdown, accompanied by James Ogilvie, their honorary medical officer. A line of them, including Ogilvie, fired five rounds at targets 25 yards away. Between them they recorded only one 'hit', a shot of Ogilvie's. A floating mine close inshore made further firing that day impossible—and no more was ever heard of the need for rifle practice.

By October 1940 a 12-inch railway-mounted howitzer of the 12th Battery 2nd Super-Heavy Regiment RA arrived on the East Kent Light Railway's farm siding at Poulton, and another at Staple Station. Both could fire on any fleet of German invasion barges which might enter Pegwell Bay. In fact, the Super-Heavies only fired once, two rounds in practice—and next day a man from the Home Office went round the village paying for the broken windows. The soldiers built a dug-out beside the line, from lengths of rail torn up from the siding. When a visiting director of the railway company expressed disapproval, he was invited to come back next day. During the night the soldiers drove the engine down the line, took up rails from another siding, and with them restored the one at Ash, to the surprise of the director on his return. It was the soldiers' practice to drive the engine to Shepherdswell for their evening pint of beer. The most important piece of equipment on every journey was the 'jack', with which to lift the engine back on to the track whenever it came off —which, owing to lack of mainte-nance of the line, it frequently did.

In June 1941 the 74th Regiment Battery moved to Goodnestone, and was relieved at Brooke House by one from the 5th Regiment, which took over the 60-pounder guns. Both batteries remained in the area long after all danger of invasion was past and, when at last their existence was remembered by the War Office, it is said that both were posted to the Far East. In October 1941, the 229th Battery of the 58th Field Artillery was stationed at Richborough Castle, and it too was equipped with antique weapons, American 75mm guns dating from 1917. Even at that critical stage of the War, the men were ordered to sift all the earth they dug from their trenches and fox-holes, so as to be sure of bringing to light any buried Roman coins.

Once more Ash Village Hall was converted into an emergency hospital, but only one military casualty was ever treated there, and it was returned to civilian use in stages from July 1943. The church tower was used both as an observation post for nearby Army units, and by the local firewatching teams. A searchlight and an anti-aircraft gun were based at Ware Farm.

Like other children elsewhere in the long hot summer of 1940, Dick and David Quested and their friends would lie for hours on the roof of a barn at Chequer unconcernedly watching aircraft in deadly combat in the skies above them. Aerial dog-fights frequently occurred high above the clouds, so that nothing could be seen, and only the sound of machine-guns heard. Spent bullets often pattered down close by, in field and orchard. An Ash man, standing in the village street watching a dog-fight in the sky above, received one through his arm. Shrapnel, particularly shell nose-cones, from the anti-aircraft guns could be dangerous. George West, who drove fruit and vegetables from Goldstone to market, was hit by a nose-cone at Shatterling and killed. Robert Chandler was luckier: he was walking in the park at Ringleton on Marrow Patrol business, carrying a hurricane-lamp, when a piece of falling shrapnel knocked the lamp out of his hand. It was locally rumoured that each newly qualified German pilot was ordered, to boost his confidence, to shoot down one of the barrage balloons above Dover, and considerable entertainment was derived in the village from watching the balloons on fire.

On Friday, 16 August 1940, a Dornier Do 17 bomber crashed south of the village, shot down by a Hurricane. The pilot and navigator, both wounded, baled out safely. The pilot was given first aid by Doris Vickers, remembering skills learnt in the VAD hospital in Ash Village Hall in the 1914-18 War. Mercy Bicker, the 61-year-old village newsagent, ran alone down Pudding Lane and arrested the navigator, brought him back to the village, and handed him over to the local policeman. The parachutes of the other two crew members failed to open, and they were killed. They were buried in Ash churchyard, and a number of villagers attended the service conducted by the vicar, Magraw. On 18 September a Messerschmitt Me 109 was shot down in flames by a Spitfire, crashing in Arthur Marchant's hop garden at Guilton; the pilot baled out severely wounded.

One day in September the local Observer Corps post spotted 348 German bombers and 617 escorting fighters, avoiding the Dover anti-aircraft defences on their way to raid London. Members of the Ash post, first established in White Post Meadow in Sandwich Road, but later moved to higher ground in New Street, became highly skilled in aircraft recognition; so good that one of them, Alec Henderson, was later seconded to serve in the Channel aboard British warships whose anti-aircraft guns were shooting down British planes by mistake.

In the early hours of 5 December, a parachute mine, fitted with a delayed-action fuse, seriously damaged Potts Farmhouse. It had landed unnoticed within 60 yards of the house, but only exploded two hours after the 'All Clear' had sounded, much to the indignation of the occupiers who had gone back to bed.

On 1 June 1942 the Germans made the first of three 'Baedeker raids' on Canterbury, in retaliation for a British raid on Cologne, and returning aircraft dropped bombs at Poulton. Next night there was another, and incendiary bombs were scattered over a wide area at Ash. On 6 June, during a third night raid on Canterbury, incendiaries were dropped at Ware, causing a fire at Downfield from which smoke from burning oil-drums drifted over Goldstone, where Jock Lennie was found walking up the road in the dark, in Home Guard uniform, carrying his rifle and wearing his gasmask, believing there had been a German gas attack. The fires of the burning city lit up the western sky, and were clearly seen from higher ground in Ash.

About midnight on Sunday, 15 August (four days before Operation 'Jubilee', the raid on Dieppe in which the Canadians suffered very heavy casualties), an Army despatch rider arrived at Ash Home Guard HQ and announced that an 'Invasion' alert was in operation. From the sound of heavy machine-gun fire, and the sight of flares and star shells, there was every indication of fierce fighting in the Stour estuary. Even the Manston anti-aircraft guns seemed to be firing almost horizontally across Pegwell Bay. At that time a detachment of the Dorset Regiment, manning pillboxes at Sandwich Bay, was billeted at Reed Barn school in Sandwich Road, Ash. One soldier had become friendly with a local girl, and she now became very concerned by his sudden disappearance, which his comrades seemed unable to explain. She was not much consoled when, six or seven months later, she received a Red Cross postcard from him, written in a German PoW camp. If German commando-type raiders did indeed land at Sandwich Bay, probably from an E-boat, seize a prisoner or two, and quickly retire, the incident does not appear to have been anywhere recorded.

On 31 October there was a fourth raid on Canterbury, this time in daylight. Because it was a Saturday afternoon, the balloon barrage was grounded. Four waves of Focke-Wolf FW 190s flew over Ash at roof-top height, firing machine-guns as they went. Bullets could be seen ricocheting off roofs all down the village street. Charlie Marsh, who was ploughing nearby on Chequer Court Farm, quietly held the heads of his alarmed pair of huge, very young horses. Three high-explosive bombs fell at Ash, and another at Richborough. At the time of the raid, Robert Chandler and Furley Spanton, after playing a game of rugger in Canterbury, were sitting in the *Fleur de Lys*, waiting to see *Gone with the Wind* at the cinema. They saw one bomb fall into the pub yard almost horizontally, and bounce out again without exploding. Chandler & Dunn's largest tractor, in Canterbury for repair, was destroyed, and they were given a permit to buy a new rubber-tyred American replacement.

At the beginning of the war, all farms were inspected by the Kent War Agricultural Executive Committee (the 'WarAg'), and classified. Those in Group A, the most efficient, were left alone; those in Group B had to obey all WarAg instructions; the WarAg took over the farming of those in Group C. At least one Ash farm, a 10-acre smallholding at Durlock, fell into Group C. Stewart Chandler from Goldstone was one of those given the unpopular task of inspecting the farms, and making sure that Class B farmers carried out instructions. The poles and railway sleepers with colliery cables threaded through them, set up in the fields to deter invading gliders, made cultivation more difficult, though much farm work was still done by hand, often with 12 or more people in a gang, walking through cereal crops hoeing, or pulling weeds, especially thistles. At Goldstone, Chandler & Dunn had four tractors, originally all steel-tyred and not allowed on roads, and seven working horses. Tractors then ran on tractor vaporising oil ('TVO'), midway between paraffin and diesel. They had to be started on petrol and, when running smoothly, switched to TVO. There was a special petrol ration for this and, by turning over to TVO rather quickly, it was possible to economise on petrol—and so have a little to spare to use in another vehicle. A series of dry winters made it possible to plough up marshes on the Ash Level but yields were low, particularly of cereals, due to poor drainage and manganese deficiency, for which at that time there was no remedy. More potatoes were grown. Farmers greatly benefited from Government fixed-prices for their produce. Before the war fruit farmers had been accustomed to getting as little as 1½d. per pound for apples; now the price for Class 1 apples (Cox, Laxton's Superb and Ellison's Orange) was fixed at 6d., and for all other varieties 3d. Besides, because agriculture had been so depressed in the 1930s, smaller farmers could elect to pay income tax on acreage, not on profits. Now, continuing to pay on an acreage basis, they had never been so well off. Food rationing was easily bearable in the country. At Goldstone, Chandler & Dunn continued to keep two or three 'house cows', and the staff ran a 'pig club'. Eggs were plentiful. Margaret Chandler went on making butter from the surplus milk, and some of it found its way to relieve hardship in the village. Labour was short on the farms. At Goldstone some of the younger men had been called up even before war broke out, either into the Reserve or as Territorials. (They mostly joined the Buffs, the East Kent Regiment, and as a result many were taken prisoner in May 1940, and spent the rest of the war in German prison camps.) Their places were taken by Land Girls, some lodging in farm cottages, some living in a Women's Land Army hostel at Elmstone Court, from where they came out to the farms daily in gangs. Eight of them worked for six months of each year for Ralphs at Guilton, in two threshing gangs. Winifred Tower and her sister Diana gave talks to new Land Girls, to warn them of the dangers facing young women in the countryside.

After all risk of invasion was past, a German PoW camp was established at Brooke House, left empty by the Army. The PoWs came out daily by lorry to work in gangs on local farms. Mostly Bavarians, older men, they were good workers. It was forbidden to pay them anything for their work, but a little cash greatly improved their output. Nor were they allowed to take anything into or out of the camp, but as Robert Chandler drove them in he would notice, flying into the bushes, little pieces of wooden fruit-boxes, which would be recovered later and carved into toys for sale. One man, who had been a schoolmaster before 1939, sent a card to Stewart and Margaret Chandler every Christmas for many years afterwards.

It was from Manston, on 12 February 1942, that six Fleet Air Arm Swordfish biplane torpedo-bombers took off, without adequate fighter escort, in a gallant but futile attempt to prevent the German battlecruisers *Scharnhorst* and *Gneisenau* and heavy cruiser

Prinz Eugen slipping through the Dover straits back to Germany. The crews knew that they were unlikely to return, and none did. The squadron commander, Lieutenant-Commander Eugene Esmonde, was awarded a posthumous Victoria Cross. Five fighter squadrons flew from Manston on 19 August to take part in the commando raid on Dieppe. It was at Manston, too, that Avro Lancaster crews received their early training for the 'Dambuster' attacks on the Ruhr dams in May 1943. Increasingly, Bomber Command and USAAF aircraft limping home from raids over Germany used Manston as an emergency landing ground. It was quite inadequate and, after a series of collisions on the airfield on 28 August 1942, orders were at last given to construct a longer runway, completed in 1944. The introduction of FIDO ('Fog Intensive Dispersal Operation') also lessened the hazards. In January 1943 a bomber crashed at Overland Farm, and a year later another, a Boeing B-17G Flying Fortress returning from a raid on Brunswick, also crash-landed there. A Hawker Typhoon from Manston crashed at Little Knell in March 1943, and another came down on the marshes below Goldstone; both pilots were killed. In June 1944, after the Allied landings in France, when the bombardment of England by V-1 flying-bombs, 'Doodlebugs', began, the RAF developed a technique for destroying them in the air, and one Manston-based squadron of Hawker Tempests claimed more than a hundred 'kills' in Operation 'Anti-Diver'. July saw the arrival at Manston of two Gloster Meteors, the first jet-engined aircraft, which also proved effective against the flying-bombs. On 16 September a V-1 was brought down in Ash, at Little Knell. Many of the aircraft and gliders taking part in the assault on the Rhine bridges at Arnhem, Operation 'Market Garden', flew from Manston on 17 September.

On 8 September, when the war seemed nearly over, the first of the V-2 long-range rockets fell, but they were aimed at London and most passed high over East Kent. The one falling nearest to Ash came down at Minster.

On Tuesday, 8 May 1945, VE Day, a 'Thanksgiving Service for the End of the European War', led jointly by the assistant curate, Walter Mahon, and the Congregational minister, Alfred Morrison, was held in the parish church, and on 15 August, VJ Day, the new vicar, Cyril Carter, and Morrison together led a joint service as a 'Victory over Japan Thanksgiving'.

Of the 11 men from the parish who were killed or died on active service during the war, 10 have been certainly identified. One was serving in the Royal Navy (October 1939), three were RAF aircrew (1941-4), and six were in the Army: four in North Africa (1942-3), one in Kent (1944) and one in Batavia in the Far East (1945). In due course, seven more names were added to the War Memorial at Ash, and four more at Westmarsh.

EIGHTEEN

THE VILLAGE SINCE 1945

After the Second World War, the Parish Council, with James Ogilvie as its new chairman (he was also chairman of the newly formed County Association of Parish Councils, and the local County Councillor) was keen to make its mark, but a decision to meet every month instead of quarterly was immediately met by the threatened resignation of the clerk (who had been in office since 1924), and hastily rescinded. It was only on the appointment of a new clerk in 1954 that the Council began to meet monthly.

The tradition of 'beating the bounds' of the parish—11 miles on foot, seven miles by boat down the river Stour—had been revived on Easter Monday 1860 by Mackarness with six men and eight boys—the first recorded occasion since 1672 and 1698—and again in May 1897 by 38 men and boys. In October 1948, at Ogilvie's suggestion, it was done again by a party of 18 which included one man who had taken part as a boy in 1897, and repeated in 1949. After a gap, it has been done every four years since 1970.

Inspired and spurred on by Ogilvie at a public meeting followed by a house-to-house collection, villagers subscribed £1,500 to enable the Parish Council to add six acres to the recreation ground in 1951. In August 1955, in answer to repeated pleas by the Parish Council, the County Council at last agreed to acquire and preserve Mount Ephraim Mill, disused since about 1928 and fast deteriorating. But it was too late: on 21 October 1955 the windmill blew down in a gale, and was destroyed.

After the war the population rose; at first slowly to 2,300 in 1951; then between 1961 and 1971 more quickly than at any time since 1821, from 2,341 to 2,615. In 1947 the District Council compulsorily purchased from Emmanuel College more Molland Farm land for housing: the first dwellings, pre-fabricated concrete 'Airey' houses, were awaiting replacement in 1999. Private houses followed, first singly then in groups. Much the biggest private building scheme in the village's history, for 66 chalet-bungalows at Glebelands, took place in the mid-1960s. The builders, based in the eastern outskirts of London, originally marketed the properties there, as country retirement homes for Londoners; not surprisingly, a number of the first buyers went back, disillusioned. The *Parish Magazine* expressed both anxiety—'Ash is growing larger and larger, with so many bungalows' (1965), and 'Whether we like it or not, in a very short time we shall no longer be a village' (1969)—and reassurance—'Those who repeatedly prophesy gloom and deplore the breakdown of village life ought to start attending such functions' (after the St Nicholas Ball, in 1965), and (less certainly) 'The Harvest Supper was reminiscent of the days when we really were a village community' (1969). In 1972 the District Council

95 Harry Marsh and 'Punch' with 'Susie', at Goss Hall in May 1953.

96   The last year of 'hopping' at Goss Hall, 1958.

opened St Nicholas House in Queen's Road, a monolithic block of very small, and soon outdated, flats for the elderly, who would be 'assured of the friendly presence of a warden'. By 1999 the warden had long gone, and the flats were difficult to let.

When the war ended much needed to be done to put the Village Hall to rights. The main hall had been returned to the Management Committee in September 1944, but the former Scout Room was retained as an ARP store until November 1945. Licences for repairs had to be obtained, a caretaker found, and displaced equipment re-assembled. 'The caretaker reported on the chairs: 69 at the Hall, 48 at the ATC headquarters, 35 at the Church Room. The 10 lent to the RA at Poulton could not be accounted for.' Later, in 1970, the Hall was improved (including a carpet for a new

'Library'), and further improved and extended in 1980 at a cost of £52,000. The Ash Women's Institute was formed in 1946; it put on a series of plays and pantomimes for several years, and kindled a new interest in local history. Ash Ladies' Hockey Club, which had prospered before the War, did not survive it; but the Bowling, Football and Cricket Clubs did, the last having a particularly successful season in 1971, and the Tennis Club rose, fell, and rose again. A Rugby Football Club was founded in 1995.

At its peak in the 1950s, the Ash Flower Show was said to attract 10,000 people to the recreation ground on the last Saturday in July, and many village organisations and local charities benefited from its profits. But with the advent of television, live high-wire acts lost their appeal, and Spanish package holidays killed the Thanet bed-and-breakfast trade from which many of the visitors to the Flower Show came. Finally it began to lose money, and the 60th Annual Show in 1964 was the last.

In the early 1950s Ash was still a busy shopping centre, with six public houses and an off-licence, two butchers, two bakers, four grocers' shops (including a Co-op) and four 'corner shops', two greengrocers, two cafés, two stationers, two hairdressers, two shoe-menders, the sub-post office, a draper, an ironmonger, a chemist, a newsagent, a coal merchant, a garage, a petrol filling station, a cycle agent, two blacksmiths, an agricultural sundriesman, two land agents, a part-time bank, part-time optician, part-time solicitor, two doctors, two veterinary surgeons, and a visiting fishmonger. There were also four other public houses in the parish: at Upper Goldstone, Hoaden, Ware, and Westmarsh, as well as the sub-post office and stores at Westmarsh.

In 1946 Leslie Moss set up as a dairymen, acquired from Molland and White Post Farms their milk rounds, and soon had rounds in Sandwich, Woodnesborough, and Eastry as well as Ash. In 1966 Vyes extended their Ash grocery; in 1967 Alan Donaldson moved his Central Garage to new larger premises on the edge of the village, and added a filling station; and in the early 1970s the forge at Guilton blossomed into Guilton Forge Garage. But Harry Burch, the village tailor (and postman, undertaker's bearer, and special constable), retired in 1965. Moss sold his dairy in 1972. One Ash bakery closed in the early 1960s, baking ceased at Westmarsh in 1971, and the second Ash bakery closed in 1998. One of the two butchers closed in 1978, the other in 1993. The veterinary surgery moved away to Sandwich in 1992, and the Westmarsh sub-post office and shop also closed about 1995. Over 25 years, three public houses were de-licensed; one garage and both filling-stations shut; both shoe-menders died; and the corner shops all closed. In 1999 there remained in Ash three public houses, two grocer's shops, a chemist, a newsagent, a hairdresser, a garage, the sub-post office, and a 4-doctor medical practice; and a public house at Westmarsh.

Gardner's brewery had expanded in a modest way, having bought up others in 1912 and 1927, but it still supplied only 47 'tied' houses, and in 1956 was itself taken over by Tomson & Wotton of Ramsgate. Afterwards, only ginger-beer (for which it had a high reputation) was brewed at Ash and, later, brewing ceased altogether. In 1968 the site was bought by Grahame Puttick Ltd., makers of diesel-electric generators, and the old buildings were mostly demolished. By 1972 Putticks employed more than 100 men and women, had a turnover of £2.5 million, and exported to 90 countries around the world. But they outgrew the site, and moved to Sandwich. Another similar business, Puma Power Plant Ltd., was later established there. About 1980 an old-established

Canterbury firm of organ-builders migrated to the former Cartwright School buildings in The Street, and a specialist toy-manufacturing and firework factory was set up in the 1980s off New Street.

In 1958, 290,000 tons of colliery shale were spread on the far bank of the Stour, just outside the parish boundary, to raise the ground level high enough to build Richborough Power Station, which came into operation in 1962. The three 114-megawatt generators' boilers were intended to burn 535,000 tons of coal a year, one-third of the total output of the Kent coalfield, but from the outset 10 per cent of fuel oil had to be added to ignite the coal, and the station later turned over, at first clandestinely then openly, to burn oil alone. When in 1990 it began to use 'Orimulsion', a 70-30 bitumen-water mixture from Venezuela, the high sulphur emissions brought complaints, of corroded paintwork on newly imported motor-cars nearby, but also of 'acid rain' from fruit farmers in Ash. But, long before the station closed down in the mid-1990s, local people driving home to east Kent came to recognise the familiar silhouette of its 450-ft chimney and three 330-ft cooling towers, conspicuous on the horizon from a considerable distance, with some affection. Demolition began in 1999.

On the Ash bank of the river, despite protests from the Parish Council, the landscape of the Ash Level beneath Richborough Castle was badly damaged from about 1975 by the repeated dumping of household refuse over an area of several hundred acres, and then moulding the result into 'rolling downland' quite foreign to the marshland of the Stour estuary.

Public transport declined. The East Kent Light Railway closed to passenger traffic in 1948, and altogether in 1951. During the 1970s the East Kent Road Car Co.'s Deal–Canterbury service was run down, and its service from Westmarsh through Ash to Sandwich withdrawn. The rate of increase in the population slowed again: to 2,664 in 1981 and 2,707 in 1991. Of 1,104 homes in the parish in 1981, 468 had been built since 1945; 219 of them by the District Council, and 249 privately.

The widespread break-up of landed estates after 1945 was reflected here. In 1947 Fleet and Guston Farms were sold by the Conyngham family, and Goldstone Court Farm—its first sale for almost 300 years—by the Toke estate. Brooke House, empty after the war, was pulled down about 1951, and the Godfreys' Ash estate, including the Victorian 'model' farm at Brooke Street, was dispersed. Many of the big old farmhouses in the parish—Molland, Chequer, Uphousden, Wingham Barton, Paramour Grange, Great Weddington, Lower Weddington, Guston, Moat and King's End—were sold away from their farms.

Increasingly, new residents of the parish, in houses large and small, were not bound economically to it, but were retired or earning their living elsewhere. Nevertheless, some quickly became leaders among the village community. Unhappily, too many others, contributing nothing to its life and getting very little in return, arrived and departed again almost unnoticed.

The development after the war of motor-lorry services, which put Ash's compara-tively small farms within an easy night's journey of the London markets, encouraged the growing of hard and soft fruit and market garden crops, though the low rainfall, averaging 22 inches a year, meant that soft fruit and vegetables increasingly needed irrigation. In 1951 there were about 1,000 acres of fruit and about 900 acres of market garden crops

97 'The Mummers' Play', performed by Ash Women's Institute, *c.*1954.

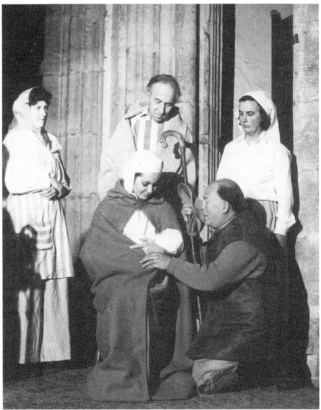

98 'The Nativity', in Ash parish church, *c.*1970.

and potatoes in the parish, 101 acres of hops (only down from 118 in 1835), about 350 cows and in-calf heifers, and about 900 sheep. Thomas Coleman employed 30 men on about 300 acres at Goss Hall and Weddington until after 1939, but as horses gave place to tractors the number fell sharply; the last working horse there was retired about 1955, and by 1999 only two men were needed. The Ash & District Rat & Sparrow Club was finally wound up about 1950; combine harvesters had done away with stacked corn, and the Club could no longer recruit working members. In 1970 the 4th-year pupils of the Cartwright School reported that among their fathers only one in eight worked on a farm, and more than half in a factory, office or laboratory. Yet, even in 1979 more than a quarter of the working population still got their living directly from agriculture within the parish boundary. The pattern of farming continued to change. At one time fruit farmers kept many pigs, their dung helping to swell the crops of blackcurrants and strawberries, but no longer. At Goss Hall and Weddington all 16 acres of hops were grubbed in 1959. Most of the hops elsewhere in the parish were grubbed in the 1960s, and 'hoppers' from London ceased to spend an annual fortnight here. By 1990 only one hop-garden remained, at Pedding.

In 1971, a Dutch enterprise erected at Twitham what was said to be the biggest single glasshouse unit in Europe. Under 30 acres of glass more than 50 regular workers then cut lettuce and picked tomatoes and cucumbers. In 1999 it employed around 300 people, and claimed to produce 30 per cent of all tomatoes eaten in England and 90 per cent of the fresh herbs. Ash seemed well-suited to glass: in 1973 new tomato-houses were put up at Knell Farm, and pot-plants and cut-flowers were produced in others at Durlock and Overland. In the 1970s, at Greenland Farm, a County Council smallholding, Roger Bradshaw grew 18 different vegetables on 36 acres, with cereals as a break-crop. Too remote to sell much at the farm gate, he sent his produce overnight to the London markets. Several Ash market-gardeners each had a lorry and a local shop-round. The requirement for heavier crops of hard fruit meant that traditional orchards of standard trees were steadily grubbed, and replaced by smaller trees protected by windbreaks, usually of alder.

By 1985 the largest fruit growers in the parish, Chandler & Dunn, had 3,000 tons of refrigerated cold-store capacity, and expected to produce between 2,000 and 3,500 tons of apples and pears from 436 acres of hard fruit; including 308 acres of dessert apples (Discovery, Worcester, Cox, Egremont Russet, Spartan, and Idared), 57 acres of cooking apples (Bramley and Grenadier), and nine acres of plums (Czar, Giant Prune, Marjorie's Seedling and Victoria); and 24 acres of soft fruit: nine acres of gooseberries (Careless), 14 acres of strawberries (Favourite, Domanil, Hapil, Korona and Bogota), and an acre of redcurrants. They farmed a total of 1,271 acres, including some in Preston and Wingham parishes; and had 36 full-time and 33 regular part-time employees.

A small commercial vineyard was established in 1978 at Moat Farm, selling its first wine in 1982. It was followed by two others. But, at the most northerly latitude at which grapes can ripen outdoors, competition in cold seasons from wines from warmer climates, and high British excise duty, made their survival precarious. Yet, through all the changes, Ash farming families have persisted for generations: the Lasletts probably since the 18th century; the Chandlers since 1810, and perhaps much earlier; and the Colemans at Goss Hall since 1818.

99 Beating the Bounds of the parish in 1970. The vicar traditionally accompanies his parishioners, and is always ceremonially 'bumped' at Pluck's Gutter.

The search for a suitable vicarage continued: in 1945 a Victorian villa (once a school) was bought in Chequer Lane, but this was re-sold in 1990 as inadequate, and a modern house purchased in Queen's Road. About 1984, the Congregational Church built a new manse in the garden of the old one in Chequer Lane, which was then sold.

In the parish church, Willement's stained-glass east window, its strong colours out of fashion, was (with the approval of the Diocesan Advisory Committee) destroyed in 1951—a few fragments survive in a tower window at Godmersham church—and the brass Communion rail replaced in oak. About 1961 the plaster was stripped from beneath the Molland chancel's medieval oak roof. The parish church's first Christian Stewardship campaign in January 1966, during which 265 families were visited, gave birth to a village playgroup and emergency car service; it also increased the church's income by two and a half times. The eight church bells were again re-hung, and two more added, in 1978. In 1967 the parish of Westmarsh was reunited with Ash, and its church closed in 1970 (and was sold and converted into a dwelling). Use of the mission rooms at Richborough and Goldstone ceased in 1969 and 1979, and the Methodist chapel at Westmarsh closed.

In 1972, when local government was being reorganised, the Parish Council unsuccessfully asked that Ash should be included in a new district based on Canterbury, rather than Dover with which it had no links or affinity.

Ash celebrated 700 years as a separate parish in 1982. The church choir and other singers from the village had already joined in a BBC television 'Songs of Praise', recorded in St Mary's Church at Sandwich and broadcast on Sunday, 27 September 1981, which attracted a record audience of 8,100,000. A Festival Fortnight in June 1982 included a concert of choral music and a flower festival in the church, a production of 'On Monday Next' and a recital of Kentish prose and poetry in the Village Hall, a barrel-rolling relay, a carnival and fête, a pageant by the Cartwright School children, an exhibition of old photographs, and much else. 'By coincidence', Ash also won that year's county 'Best Kept Village' competition.

In the 1970s calls for an Ash by-pass grew louder. A by-pass for Sandwich, passing through the eastern part of Ash parish, opened in 1980. Ash Street, in several places little more than 15 feet wide between buildings, was said to be the narrowest stretch of A-road in the country. In 1984, 7,000 vehicles a day, expected to increase to 8,200 by the year 2000, passed through it, and the County Council placed Ash 4th (out of 26) in its priority list. The Parish Council's 1985 Village Appraisal, pressing for a by-pass, won one of 10 national 'Living Village' awards. (The £125 prize was spent on a weather-vane for the Village Hall.) In December 1986 the County Council exhibited four possible routes for a by-pass, but by the summer of 1988 nothing more seemed to have been done. There were increasing complaints of damage to older properties in The Street; flexible bollards on the narrow pavements were destroyed more quickly than they were replaced. The County Council assured Jonathan Aitken, the local MP, that Ash retained its position in the programme, but then news of the intended construction of an Eastry by-pass (actually begun in 1989) caused further annoyance. In June 1990 the County Council at last applied for planning permission to construct the Ash by-pass, and in December made compulsory purchase orders for the land needed, but too late for an award of government Transport Supplementary Grant for 1991-2. Then, against all local expectations, it was not included in the County Council's own transport budget for 1991-2. Ash people were furious; a By-pass Campaign was set up, with a fund-raising 'soup kitchen'. One demonstration, on 9 January 1991, at which more than 150 villagers turned out, and traffic was held up for half an hour, ended in a scuffle during which, after a lorry-driver shouted abuse, three elderly villagers were knocked down. Mary Smith, a district councillor for Ash, ceremonially burned County Council papers 'full of broken promises'. These displays of feeling, mostly by women, attracted considerable radio, TV and newspaper publicity. It was clear that the County Council's preparations were so far behind that construction could not start before 1992-3. Worse, originally first in the County Council's priority list for 1992-3, Ash now slipped to second place. Mary Smith and Bill Henderson, candidates for the District Council election in April 1991, said in their 'manifesto' that one senior County Council officer involved had confessed that he had never been to Ash. In July Lady Pender, the local county councillor, told the County Council: 'The local residents are shattered. They don't know whom to trust. I have been promised action, but the by-pass is now as uncertain as ever. What am I to tell them, and why should they believe me?'

'Despite repeated public and written assurances from county councillors and officers that nothing would move us from first place', declared Mary Smith, 'we have been let down again.' Local anger was so evident that additional police were drafted in for the opening of the Eastry by-pass in June 1991. At another demonstration in The Street a police inspector, two sergeants and three constables were openly (and embarrassedly) present, with reserves hidden in vans. The Ash women, though amused that their displays of feeling had engendered an apparent belief in high places that the village 'is seething with potentially violent agitators', felt they scarcely deserved this attention. 'Your local officers, left to their own devices, hardly trouble us at all. They are indeed rarely visible, and have given a new meaning to the term 'sleeping policemen' in this part of rural Kent.'

Meanwhile, during the nine-day public inquiry into the compulsory purchase orders, which began on 2 July, all objections to the chosen route were withdrawn. On Monday, 16 December, Aitken met the Prime Minister, John Major, and they discussed the Ash by-pass. Later the same day, after talking to Christopher Chope, the Minister for Roads and Traffic, Aitken reported only that he was 'cautiously optimistic', but there was little surprise in Ash when, on Thursday, 19 December, Aitken was chosen to ask the Secretary of State for Transport, Malcolm Rifkind, to announce in the House of Commons the allocation of Transport Supplementary Grant for local roads for 1992-3, or when, in his reply, Rifkind announced that Ash by-pass was third in the national list.

On 19 May 1992 work began on the 3½-mile road, estimated to cost £3,900,000. Within a year, on St George's Day 1993, it was open. On Sunday 13 June the village celebrated with, among other jollifications, a street party held, appropriately, in the narrowest part of The Street. But, although the new road achieved its purpose of taking much of the through traffic from The Street, it also cut off all the smaller settlements to the north from the main village, so that there must still be doubt whether it would not have been better routed south of the village. It may also have hastened the demise of some village shops.

Ash received two notable charitable bequests in 1989 and 1994; from Jack Foat, an Ash fruit-grower who died in 1978, and from Frank Kingsland, who died in 1994 and whose father had been the schoolmaster at Westmarsh from 1913 to 1938. Both left the residue of their estates for charitable purposes in the parish. Jack Foat's Trust has been able to lay out two pieces of land, totalling 17 acres, for informal recreation, and Frank Kingsland's executors to set up a new almshouse trust with two bungalows, and find money to re-build Westmarsh Village Hall in 1995; and both trusts continue to make grants to village organisations.

The District Council's 1996 draft Local Plan was, after a public enquiry, criticised in July 1999 by a Government inspector for failing to take account of rural communities' housing and other needs. Commenting that Ash was undoubtedly an important rural centre where there was local support for growth, and on the need to house the expected large increase in those working at Pfizer's pharmaceutical manufacturing plant (first established north of Sandwich in 1954, much enlarged, and expanding fast), he recommended that Ash should be recognised as 'capable of accommodating more than minor growth in response to its needs and available facilities', and that development of enough additional land for 85 dwellings should be allowed. It is too soon to predict what effect this will have on the parish in the next 10 years, and beyond.

Select Bibliography

I Manuscript sources

Ash parish archives: including Parish Registers 1558 to date; Vestry Minutes 1704 to
date; Churchwardens' Accounts 1635-1711 and 1727-1922; Records of the Overseers
of the Poor (accounts 1601-10, 1668-1720, 1734-1833; settlement certificates 1697-
1818; affiliation orders 1697-1818; removal orders 1724-1818, apprenticeship inden-
tures 1635-1812; workhouse accounts 1818, 1827-32, etc.) Highway Surveyors' accounts
1726-1841; Cartwright School trustees accounts 1726-1841, minutes 1834-75; Kelsey
School trustees accounts 1860-1939, minutes 1860-75; Tithe Map and Apportionment
1842.

Centre for Kentish Studies, Maidstone: Hearth Tax assessments 1662 and 1664; Consistory
Court wills and inventories; North MSS; Neame MSS.

Canterbury Cathedral Library: Archdeacon's Court and Consistory Court depositions,
comperta et detecta.

Lambeth Palace: Parliamentary Survey MSS.

II Periodicals

Ash Parish Magazine 1899-1917, a few odd copies 1918-63 and 1964-99

Kentish Gazette 1817–

East Kent Mercury

III Contemporary works of reference

Bagshaw's *Directory of Kent* 1848

Kelly's *Directory of Kent* 1870, 1878, 1899, 1907, 1918, 1924, 1930, 1934

Dover Illustrated, with some account of the Villages of Ash, Wingham and Eastry (Gravesend,
n.d. but of 1899)

Ash Village Appraisal (Ash Parish Council) 1986

IV Other printed sources

Boys, John, *A General View of the Agriculture of Kent*, 1796 (2nd ed. 1813)

Chalklin, C.W., ed., *The Compton Census of 1676, the Dioceses of Canterbury and Rochester*
(Kent Records XVII) 1960

Chalklin, C.W., ed., *The Kent Lay Subsidy Roll of 1334-5* (Kent Records XVIII) 1964

Colvin, H.M., ed., *A list of the Archbishop of Canterbury's tenants by knight service in the
reign of Henry II* (Kent Records XVIII, KAS) 1964

Cotton, Charles, ed., *Canterbury Chantries and Hospitals in 1546* (Kent Records XII, supplement) 1934

Douglas, D.C., ed., *The Domesday Monachorum of Christ Church, Canterbury* (R.H.S. London) 1944

Du Boulay, F.R.H., ed., Calendar of the demesne leases made by Archbishop Warham 1503-32 (Kent Records XVIII) 1964

Garrod, G.H., *A survey of the Agriculture of Kent* (Royal Agricultural Society, London) 1954

Gleig, G.R., *Personal Reminiscences of the 1st Duke of Wellington*, ed. Mary E. Gleig (Edinburgh) 1904

Hussey, Arthur, ed., *Ash Wills* (Archaeologia Cantiana XXXIV-XXXVII) (London) 1920-5

Hussey, Arthur, ed., *Kent Chantries* (Kent Records XII) 1934-6

Hussey, Arthur, ed., *Kent Obit and Lamp Rents* (Kent Records XIV) 1936

Philipot, John, *A Book of Church Notes*, ed. C.R. Councer (Kent Records XVII) 1960

Virgoe, R., ed., A*ncient Indictments in King's Bench referring to Kent 1450-52* (Kent Records XVIII, KAS) 1964

Whatmore, L.E., ed., Archdeacon Harpsfield's Visitation 1557, together with visitations of 1556 and 1558 (Catholic Record Society XLV-XLVI) 1951

Woodcock, Audrey M., ed., *Cartulary of the Priory of St Gregory, Canterbury*, (R.H.S. Camden Third Series LXXXVIII) 1956

V Secondary works

Armstrong, N., *The Economy of Kent 1640-1914* (Maidstone) 1995

Bentwich, Helen C., *History of Sandwich* (Sandwich) 1971

Boys, William, *Collections for an History of Sandwich in Kent* (Canterbury) 1792

Bushe-Fox, J.P., Excavation of the Roman Fort at Richborough (1st, 2nd, 3rd, 4th Reports); ed. B.W. Cunliffe (5th Report), (Society of Antiquaries of London) 1926-68

Bushe-Fox, J.P., *Richborough Castle* (HMSO) 1938

Butler, Robert, *Richborough Port* (Ramsgate) 1993, rev. ed. 1999

Camden, William, *Britannia, Kent*, ed. Richard Gough 1789, ed. Gordon G. Copley (London) 1977

Canterbury Archaeological Trust, The Ash By-pass 1992, Interim Report (*Arch. Cant.* CXII) 1993

Catt, A.R., *The East Kent Railway* (Tarrant Hinton, Blandford) 1975

Champion, T. and Ogilvie, J.D., 'A late Bronze-age hoard from Hoaden, Kent' (*Arch. Cant.* XCVII) 1981

Coles Finch, William, *Watermills and Windmills* (London) 1933

Collyer, David G., *Battle of Britain Diary, East Kent, July-Sept. 1940* (Deal) 1980

Collyer, David G., *Deal and District at War 1939-45* (Stroud) 1995

Course, Edwin, *Railways of Southern England, Independent and Light Railways* (London) 1976

Croft, Justin, 'An Assault on the Royal Justices at Ash, etc.' (*Arch. Cant.* CXVII) 1997

Du Boulay, F.R.H., *The Lordship of Canterbury* (London) 1966

Ellis Davidson, Hilda R. and Webster, Leslie, 'The Anglo-Saxon Burial at Coombe' (*Mediaeval Archaeology* XI) 1967

Faussett, Bryan, *Inventorium Sepulchrale*, ed. C. Roach Smith, (London) 1856

Gardiner, Dorothy, *Companion into Kent* (London) 1934

Gardiner, Dorothy, *Historic Haven, The Story of Sandwich* (Derby) 1934

Gardner & Co. Ltd., A few places of interest in a 'Corner of Kent' (Ash) (n.d. but 1937)

Glover, Judith, *The Place-names of Kent* (London) 1976

Goodsall, R.H., *Church of St Nicholas at Ash* (*Arch. Cant.* XXXI) 1915

Grieve, Hilda E.P., *The Deprived Married Clergy in Essex 1553-61* (R.H.S. 4th Series XXII) 1940

Hammond, J.L. and B., *The Village Labourer* (London) 1911

Hasted, Edward, *The History and Topographical Survey of the County of Kent* (Canterbury) 1st (folio) ed. 1778-99; 2nd (octavo) ed. 1797-1801

Hearne, C.M., Perkins, D.R.J. and Andrews, P., 'The Sandwich Bay Wastewater Treatment Scheme Archaeological Project, 1992-94' (*Arch. Cant.* CXV) 1995

Hicks, Alison J., 'Excavations at Each End, Ash, 1992' (*Arch. Cant.* CXVIII) 1998

Hobsbawm, E.J. and Rudé, George, *Captain Swing* (London) 1969

Hussey, Arthur, *Chronicles of Wingham* (Canterbury) 1896

Igglesden, Charles, *A saunter through Kent with pen and pencil* XVIII (Ashford) 1925

Johnson, J.S., *Richborough and Reculver* (English Heritage) 1991

Lyne, R.M., *Military Railways in Kent* (Maidstone) 1983

McCall Smith, Danvers, 'Ash-next-Sandwich' (Official Guide of Ash Parish Council), (London) (n.d. but *c.*1925)

Margary, I.D., 'Notes on Roman Roads in East Kent' (*Arch. Cant.* LXI) 1948

Mitchell, Vic and Smith, Keith, *The East Kent Light Railway* (Midhurst) 1989

Newman, Anthea E., 'The Old Poor Law in East Kent, 1606-1834' (Kent Ph.D. thesis) 1970

Newman, Anthea E., 'Removal and Settlement in the parish of Ash 1670-1834' (*Cantium* II) 1970

Newman, John, *North East and East Kent* (*Buildings of England* ed. N. Pevsner) (London) 3rd ed. 1983

O(gilvie), D.J.R., 'James Davis Ogilvie' (*Arch. Cant.* CXV) 1995

Panton, F.H., 'The Canterbury-Richborough Roman Road, a review' (*Arch. Cant.* CXIV) 1994

Parfitt, Keith, Ash 1992 Mill Field Archaeological Watching Brief Report (Dover Archaeological Group) (typescript) 1993

Parish, W.D. and Shaw, W.F., *Dictionary of Kentish Dialect* (London) 1887

Parkin, E.W., 'Wingham, a medieval town' (*Arch. Cant.* XCVIII) 1977

Perkins, D.R.J., 'The Hoaden (II) Bronze hoard' (*Arch. Cant.* CXVIII) 1998

Planché, James Robinson, *A Corner of Kent* (London) 1864

Rady, Jonathan, The Ash by-pass (Canterbury Archaeological Trust 17th Annual Report) 1993

Reaney, P.H., 'Place-names and early settlement in Kent' (*Arch. Cant.* LXXVI) 1961

Smith, R.A.L. *Canterbury Cathedral Priory, a study in monastic administration* (Cambridge) 1943

Southworth, Edmund, ed., for National Museums on Merseyside, *Anglo-Saxon Cemeteries, a reappraisal* (Stroud) 1990

Stockman, Rocky, *The History of the Royal Air Force, Manston 1916-1986* (Manston) 1986

Tower, Sir Reginald, 'The Family of Septvans' (*Arch. Cant.* XL) 1928

Tower, Sir Reginald, *The Church of St Nicholas at Ash* (Ash) 1928 (rev. ed. D.G. Downes, 1972)

Wallenburg, J.K., *Kentish Place Names* (Uppsala) 1931

Wallenburg, J.K., *The Place-names of Kent* (Uppsala) 1934

Ward, Gordon, 'The lists of Saxon churches in the Domesday Monachorum and White Book of St Augustine's' (*Arch. Cant.* XLV) 1933

Yates, Nigel, Hume, Robert and Hastings, Paul, *Religion and Society in Kent 1640-1914* (Maidstone) 1994

INDEX

Illustration page numbers are indicated by bold type